theatre & animals

Lourdes Orozco

palgrave
macmillan

First published 2013 by
PALGRAVE MACMILLAN

Palgrave Macmillan in the UK is an imprint of Macmillan
Publishers Limited, registered in England, company number
785998, of Houndmills, Basingstoke, Hampshire RG21 6XS.

Palgrave Macmillan in the US is a division of St Martin's Press LLC,
175 Fifth Avenue, New York, NY 10010.

Palgrave Macmillan is the global academic imprint of the above
companies and has companies and representatives throughout
the world.

Palgrave® and Macmillan® are registered trademarks in the United
States, the United Kingdom, Europe and other countries

ISBN: 978–0–230–36143–0 paperback

This book is printed on paper suitable for recycling and made
from fully managed and sustained forest sources. Logging,
pulping and manufacturing processes are expected to conform to
the environmental regulations of the country of origin.

A catalogue record for this book is available from the British
Library.

A catalog record for this book is available from the Library of
Congress.

contents

series editors' preface

The theatre is everywhere, from entertainment districts to the fringes, from the rituals of government to the ceremony of the courtroom, from the spectacle of the sporting arena to the theatres of war. Across these many forms stretches a theatrical continuum through which cultures both assert and question themselves.

Theatre has been around for thousands of years, and the ways we study it have changed decisively. It's no longer enough to limit our attention to the canon of Western dramatic literature. Theatre has taken its place within a broad spectrum of performance, connecting it with the wider forces of ritual and revolt that thread through so many spheres of human culture. In turn, this has helped make connections across disciplines; over the past fifty years, theatre and performance have been deployed as key metaphors and practices with which to rethink gender, economics, war, language, the fine arts, culture and one's sense of self.

Theatre & is a long series of short books which hopes to capture the restless interdisciplinary energy of theatre and performance. Each book explores connections between theatre and some aspect of the wider world, asking how the theatre might illuminate the world and how the world might illuminate the theatre. Each book is written by a leading theatre scholar and represents the cutting edge of critical thinking in the discipline.

We have been mindful, however, that the philosophical and theoretical complexity of much contemporary academic writing can act as a barrier to a wider readership. A key aim for these books is that they should all be readable in one sitting by anyone with a curiosity about the subject. The books are challenging, pugnacious, visionary sometimes and, above all, clear. We hope you enjoy them.

Jen Harvie and Dan Rebellato

foreword

In 2003, I went to see Alain Platel's *Wolf* in Duisburg. A pack of dogs roamed among the performers. Sometimes they drifted offstage into the vast factory space of the Kraftzentrale. The audience coaxed them back on. Maybe I was reminded of the toddler in Platel's *Iets op Bach*, wandering between the legs of the dancers, sometimes ignored, sometimes attended to, before she returns to her mattress at the back of the space. And I probably thought about those guard dogs straining to get at the dancers in the field of carnations in Pina Bausch's *Nelken* in Edinburgh eight years earlier.

> All animals are different, but all share the ability to prompt considerations around humans and their relationship to the other, as well as around the theatre and its capacity to destabilise the real.

So writes Lourdes Orozco in *Theatre & Animals*. It's a smart, provocative and timely insight into the history and current practice of working with animals in theatre. Orozco confronts crucial questions around the relationship between humanity and animality in and through performance, citing a wealth of examples – from anthropomorphism in Disney's *The Lion King* to the 'chaotic multispecies encounter' of Jan Fabre's *Parrots and Guinea Pigs*.

For almost thirty years I've made theatre with people who have never done it before. I've worked with philosophers, families, soldiers, chefs, children, florists, cleaners and countless others – as well as actors, dancers, musicians and opera singers. I'm attracted both to the virtuosic and the transparently raw in performance, and to that sense that whoever is onstage is comfortable with being uncomfortable in front of us. It means that my work seems to have a brittle quality, a tendency to feel like it might collapse in on itself, a sense of genuine uncertainty. I'm happy with that.

Like most devising processes, ours is one in which material is generated or gathered over time, and – after a period of sifting, selecting and editing – begins to coalesce. Through repetition, it settles and compacts. Like gravel. Where fragments might initially have raised sparks in their unpredictable collisions, over time they sink into place next to each other. Rhythms and reactions become familiar, learned.

So I try to introduce agents of disruption into performance. I'm interested in what happens when the figures onstage appear to be unaware of the rules and structures of the event. Or at least I'm interested in what happens when we make that assumption. This has led to my working frequently with young children and with animals. I ask myself (and the audience?) what this means in relation to the world outside the theatre as well as within, about questions of agency and the ethics of responsibility at play. My own sense of knowing that the figure onstage is 'comfortable with being uncomfortable' is challenged.

In Quarantine's work, animals and children hang out in rehearsal alongside everybody else. They appear to be happy to join in our games. Sometimes they even want to do the same thing again the next day. Often what happens during the breaks in rehearsal ends up as onstage activity.

For *Old People, Children and Animals* (2008), I gathered together two three-year-old girls, four untrained women and a man in their sixties and seventies, an intensely teenage girl rock band, seven white rabbits and a parrot called Betty. At one end of the marquee space was a small raised platform stage, backed by a silver slash curtain, with a single red plastic chair. Before the audience entered, Betty's handler placed her on the chair. To start the show, our production manager positioned a microphone in front of her. Then we all waited. To hear what she might say.

For the first couple of performances Betty sat, impassive, ruffling her wings, occasionally turning her back on us.

Pretty soon the parrot became familiar with the routine of the show. She heard Chloe, the ace drummer in the band, enter the backstage corridor with a sackful of mechanical rabbits. The real ones came later. Chloe and Betty spent time together in rehearsal and were familiar with each other. After three or four performances, Betty began to squawk 'Chloe' as soon as she heard the drummer approach. The sound was parrot-like — what else? — but quite distinctly that name. This then happened every night, at the same moment. It was a line that the parrot devised for herself and repeated.

So much for disruption ...

Richard Gregory is an artistic director of Quarantine (www.qtine.com).

theatre & animals

Introduction: a night in the theatre

In 2001, Rodrigo García's play *After Sun* was performed by invitation at the Sitges Teatre Internacional festival, an event staged in Sitges (near Barcelona) before an international audience. *After Sun* was García's first visit to the region of Catalonia, and I was there to see it. Half-way into the performance actor Juan Loriente put on a Mexican wrestling mask, brought a cardboard box out to centre stage and started dancing frantically to Tom Jones' 'Sex Bomb'. Suddenly he opened the box, and out came two white rabbits, which Loriente grabbed by their necks. He then proceeded to whisk the animals into the air and to mime sexual acts with them. The audience became uneasy. The people sitting close to me whispered complaints. The presence of the rabbits was perceived to be wrong; their treatment by Loriente, and ultimately by García, abusive. After a while, some members of the audience walked out of the theatre, asking the actor to stop what he was doing as they left. 'Animals!' one viewer shouted from the back of the theatre as an insult to the actor and García's creative team. In her desire to castigate the actor, she turned to the insult 'animal'. In this spectator's view, the animals were positioned as victims in the hands of the human, whose violent, uncontrolled behaviour was deemed animal-like. Her complaint exposed the complex and paradoxical nature of human–animal relations, marked at once by love and neglect in equal measure.

After this short upheaval, and with two-thirds of the audience left in the theatre, the production reached its final scene, in which Loriente and actor–dancer Patricia Lamas appeared as manager and trainee in a McDonald's kitchen. Lamas, the trainee, was being taught how to cook the perfect hamburger. The audience watched without complaint. No one expressed disgust at animal meat being cooked onstage. The spectators could not relate to the body of an animal that was no longer visible. The animal had become food, and that, somehow, seemed more acceptable than the mistreatment of the live rabbits. Later, I found out that during the tour of *After Sun* the director had invariably been approached by audience members asking him about the fate of the rabbits at the end of each performance. Some people offered to take them home; others saw them as free dinner. *After Sun*'s rabbits were at once beloved pets, food, unwilling performers and mere objects.

In *Animal* (2002), Erica Fudge highlights these contradictions by suggesting that 'we rarely make the connection between the cat we live with and the cow we eat' (pp. 9–10).

Fudge reminds us that 'through their appearance in fables, children's books and films [rabbits] have acquired qualities that have enabled a transformation from animal in general to individual in particular' (p. 38). Rabbits sit particularly uncomfortably in this intersection, and the ones in García's production embodied the complex – and often contradictory – relationships between humans and (other) animals, representing centuries of shared histories and cohabitation.

Since that night, my theatre-going experience has been marked by similar instances of animal performance, as animal presence has become a regular feature of experimental theatre practices in contemporary Europe. Thinking about the numerous animals that I have seen onstage, I realised that the history of human–animal relations runs parallel with animal presence and participation in performance practices from cave paintings to contemporary rodeos. In performance, animals raise questions about the status of both the human and the animal and about the relationship between the two. They transform theatre's relationship with representation by appearing as a real presence onstage; they challenge its meaning-making processes and invite a reassessment of the ways in which theatre is produced, received and disseminated. The presence of the animal in performance also produces a necessary engagement with ethics and exposes theatre's negotiations with political, social and economic questions, with policymaking and with labour laws. This book addresses some of these issues.

Theatre & Animals is centrally concerned with animal representation in performance contexts, whether this means the live presence of real animals, metaphorical allusions to animals or the use of animal puppets, images and other forms of representation. These differences matter, as every animal and each specific performance experience poses a new set of questions. Furthermore, the various ways in which animals appear in performance raise different ethical questions. Live animals – and especially those with whom humans have long-established relationships, such as dogs, horses and cats – might trigger empathy and in turn concerns about their treatment on- and offstage in a way that puppets do not (although puppets, cartoon characters, stuffed animals and furries – fur suits representing anthropomorphised animals, such as those used at Disney World – can point towards problematic human–animal interactions based in the centrality of the human). Moreover, live animals onstage might bring risk and danger in ways that non-live animals do not (although the presence of the latter instead of the former might be a form of resistance or challenge to – or, indeed, a strategy to bypass – health-and-safety regulations, risk assessments and other forms of policing). All animals are different, but all share the ability to prompt considerations around humans and their relationship to the other, as well as around the theatre and its capacity to destabilise the real.

Theatre & Animals tackles these topics via a journey through contemporary theatre and performance practice. While it attempts to be comprehensive, the scope of the book is necessarily constrained by its length. It centres on contemporary Western practices, and this focus provides the book with its examples and informs its philosophical and political approaches to animals and performance. The book engages with the most productive performance interventions with respect to questions of human–animal subjectivity; ethics; risk, labour and economics; and representation.

Animals in performance contexts require an engagement with other research fields outside theatre and performance. Thus, my approach is necessarily interdisciplinary and engages with work in the area of animal studies, a research field that is concerned with the idea of the animal, its relationship with the human and its positioning within human societies. Animal studies has demonstrated how animals have been central to human cultural history and thought for centuries. The book not only presents an account of animals in performance but also explores performance's interaction with the questions raised by the other disciplines – primarily philosophy, history and the visual arts – encapsulated in animal studies.

Furthermore, my interest is not only in the animal per se, or in human–animal interactions in performance contexts, but also in the challenges that the animal poses to performance. Examining the presence of animals provides an opportunity to investigate how performance in general works and how it has long played a part in human–animal relations.

Theatre and performance studies within animal studies

In *Zoographies* (2008), Matthew Calarco explains how the two main topics of concern in animal studies could be summarised as 'the being of animals or "animality"' and 'the human-animal distinction' (p. 2). Theatre and performance studies scholars have made productive contributions to these two overarching themes. Methodologies from performance analysis have been applied to popular performance practices such as fox hunting, bullfighting, rodeo riding, sheep herding and bear baiting (a form of entertainment in which a bear whose claws and teeth have been removed is put into an arena – a bear garden – with well-trained hunting dogs). In addition, the presence of animals has triggered considerations about their participation in the theatre economy, their training and their ability to act. Above all, it has highlighted ethical and moral questions about their agency and their objectification. Some attention has also been paid to how animals are represented in performance and how these representations relate to their status in broader societal contexts.

One of the most productive developments at the intersection of theatre studies and animal studies has been Una Chaudhuri's concept of zooësis, which refers to the way in which culture makes art and meaning with the figure and body of the animal. It has been explored in two articles ('Animal Geographies', 2003, and '(De)Facing the Animals', 2007) and in the publications emerging from the New York University-based 'The Animal Project' (begun in 2006). Most importantly, the concept has influenced the study of animals in performance and the positioning of performance within animal studies. In her 2007 article, Chaudhuri explains that performance studies has a duty to engage with animals because of the multiple examples of human–animal interactions that are 'imbued with the traits of performance – embodiment, presence, expressive encounters in shared time and space' (p. 9). She defines zooësis as an attempt to document these encounters and to chart the presence of animals in literature, theatre and drama, popular culture and popular performance.

As the works listed in the further reading section at the end of this book suggest, animals are a productive starting-point to study theatre and performance practices, and looking at animals in these contexts helps us better understand their role in human societies and cultural histories.

A note on language

While the language that humans use to think, talk and write about animals is often another example of the naturalisation of human exceptionalism and a way to exercise it, it can also constitute the first step towards change, an opportunity to destabilise the status quo. For this reason, and in order to show how this book participates in the ongoing ethical and political debates in animal studies, I need to explain my choice of terms when talking about animals. My use of the plural 'animals' and the singular 'the animal' engages with Jacques Derrida's concerns around the use of the general singular 'the Animal' in his 2008 text *The Animal That Therefore I Am* (p. 41); the reason this book is not titled *Theatre & the Animal* is to avoid falling into the linguistic trap in which a singular noun represents all animals in general, except for the human being.

In agreement with Cary Wolfe's terminological explanations in his book *Animal Rites* (2003), I have used the terms 'animal' and 'human' instead of the commonly used terms 'non-human animal' and 'human animal' throughout the book. As Wolfe explains, 'the term "animal" should always be taken to mean the more technically accurate, but stylistically infelicitous, term "non-human animal"' (p. 209).

While I acknowledge that animals are individuals and that their sex matters, I have decided to use the pronoun 'it' rather than 'he' or 'she' when referring to individual animals. Like Wolfe, I do so 'recognizing that … speaking of the animal with the neuter pronoun is a barometer of our inability to take seriously the possibility of the animal's nongeneric being' (p. 209).

Finally, the book uses the terms 'theatre' and 'performance' to signal the distinctions between performance that happens in theatres and uses theatrical elements such as a playtext and performances that take place in other locations, such as circus tents, aqua parks and rodeo and bullfighting arenas. I recognise this division in my treatment of theatre studies and performance studies as two separate but linked disciplines.

Animals in art, spectacle and text: a brief history

Animals have always been an aspect of human experience, and they feature in the earliest forms of representational art. The first artistic representations, accounts of rituals and religious texts narrating the origin of human life on Earth document what we know of early human–animal interaction. When animals began to be hunted for food and tamed for labour, sustenance and companionship, they also entered the human imagination and artistic practice. Their role in performance practice can likewise be traced back to prehistoric times. Early cave paintings demonstrate the crucial status of animals in shamanistic rituals, community gatherings and hunting demonstrations. As Linda Kalof explains in *Looking at Animals in Human History* (2007), these Palaeolithic representations of animals were central to community life: 'groups joined together from time to time for ceremony, ritual, painting and the exchange of important information about the movement of animals' (p. 6). Kalof highlights the sophisticated techniques used by the artists of the Chauvet caves in the south of France (30,000 BC), which 'render the animals spectacularly lifelike', conveying a sense of 'body motion, speed, strength and power' (p. 1). These images are extremely difficult to access, but they can be seen in Werner Herzog's *Cave of Forgotten Dreams* (2011), a film that emphasises the centrality of the animal in the origins of art.

In antiquity, animals – whether live or represented – continued to occupy a vital place in human communities. Examples in visual art represent human–animal interaction in environments both domestic and outdoor (hunting, fighting, labouring and racing). Arguing that the centrality of animals to human life extended beyond the undertaking of necessary tasks, Kalof explains how Mesopotamian art included animal carvings on musical instruments, depicting 'scenes of intertwined heroic humans and animals, human-headed bulls and animals performing human behaviors such as playing musical instruments' (p. 14). These early carvings demonstrate that the idea of the animal as a performer was already present in this early culture, and the animal's participation in human-led entertainment became increasingly visible in later ages. Furthermore, these carvings are particularly interesting for their portrayal of animals performing human behaviours, which became a central part of their role in the entertainment industries from the nineteenth century onwards, as Peta Tait's book *Wild and Dangerous Performances* (2012) demonstrates. These early representations began a process of associations being made between human and animal characteristics, concepts and ideas. (In Mesopotamia, for instance, the bull was already linked to strength.) These associations are still current in contemporary societies and have consequently permeated performance practice. For example, the link between animals and fear, the wild and the uncontrollable is a fascination that has come to define human–animal interactions in performance and beyond.

Animals were also at the heart of the ancient Greek and Roman cultures. Beyond their place in daily life as sources of food and labour, it was during these periods that their role in entertainment became central to religious festivals and, in Roman times, the circus. It was also in ancient Greece and Rome that the first philosophical texts on the relationship of animals to humans were written, sparking debates on human supremacy (Aristotle) and animal ethics (Plutarch) that continue to this day. As David Fraser explains in his book *Understanding Animal Welfare* (2008), Aristotle's statement that 'although humans and animals share many characteristics ... , it is humans alone that have the capacity for logos or reason' started the animal welfare debate, which remains vibrant today (p. 10).

In Greek theatre, animals could be live on the stage, represented by actors or merely mentioned as offstage presences. In his article 'Animals in the Greek Theatre' (1959), P. D. Arnott describes how, in Greek tragedy, animals were used primarily 'to produce spectacular effects' (p. 177); for example, central characters in Aeschylus' *Agamemnon*, *The Persians* and *Eumenides* and in Euripides' *Stheneboea* and *Iphigenia in Aulis* made their entrances on chariots pulled by real horses. Arnott also discusses the associations between animals and particular genres that were in place during the Greek period. Horses belonged to tragedy, while donkeys – 'familiar and undignified' animals (p. 3) – carried minor characters in comedies such as Aristophanes' *The Frogs* and *The Wasps* and Euripides' *The Birds*. However, because animals are difficult subjects to manage in the theatre, most plays were written such that, while animals were mentioned by the characters, their presence was not actually required onstage. In *The Wasps* and *The Birds*, Arnott explains, animals were most likely played by human actors, since they are required to perform on cue (p. 4). As we will see later in this book, difficulties around the unpredictability of animal performers, together with the practicalities of keeping animals in the theatre, remain an issue in contemporary theatre practice, where they have been further complicated by labour and economic considerations and, above all, ethical questions relating to animal welfare.

Animals were also part of other performance-related practices during these periods. As Kalof explains, there is evidence that both Greece and Rome continued the tradition of keeping zoos, menageries and animal parks, and of bullfights, the baiting of humans and animals, and staged hunts, all of which had been part of the Egyptian and Minoan cultures (pp. 23–37). The first pictorial testimonies of bull-fighting, for example, are to be found in Egyptian art, while the Minoan practice of bull leaping can be regarded as the origin of rodeos as they are currently performed in the Americas (pp. 33–34).

The Greeks and Romans used animals as reluctant participants in sacrificial religious festivals. Here, the animal typically embodied an expiatory soul through which the salvation of humanity was performed. In his 1979 article 'Attitudes towards Animals in Ancient Greece', Steven Lonsdale explains that the Greeks in particular 'had a tendency to interpret events and phenomena as divine signs' and 'communicated with their gods through animal sacrifices and divine bird omens' (p. 8). Similar practices and beliefs continued through to the nineteenth century in the West and can still be found today in parts of Asia and Africa. Interestingly, as Suzana Marjanić explains in her article 'The Zoostage as Another Ethical Misfiring' (2010), animal sacrifice has been reclaimed as a contemporary performance practice in the West during the twentieth and twenty-first centuries, in part as a means to produce spectacle.

In Roman times, spectacle took a sharper, more brutal turn. Gladiators – usually slaves but sometimes free-born volunteers – with various degrees of protection and forms of weaponry were made to fight wild animals such as lions, tigers and bears. During this period, animals were also trained to perform tricks for human entertainment, and were a fundamental constituent of sea and land battle recreations and the re-enactment of myths performed in Roman circuses. Romans spared no expense when putting on large spectacles, which were central to public life and an effective public display of wealth, power and status. Most of these spectacles included the participation of wild and exotic animals. Sometimes the animals were merely exhibited; at other times, they were executed for the amusement of thrill-seeking Roman spectators. Kalof relates that 'Augustus flooded the Circus Flaminius in 2 BC and exhibited thirty-six crocodiles' and 'Nero flooded a wooden amphitheatre with seawater; filled it with fish and other marine animals and staged a mock sea-battle between Athenians and Persians' (p. 37). Even Moby Doll, the first captive killer whale used for entertainment, as Fraser explains in *Understanding Animal Welfare* (pp. 2–4), had a Roman predecessor during the reign of the emperor Claudius, who also created a show using a trapped whale.

During the Middle Ages, the horse in particular became highly valued for its essential participation in labour (agriculture and war), as Elaine Walker explains in *Horse* (2008). Horses were a key element in the performance of class and status and in sports such as jousting. Other animals were also central to medieval life. For instance, as fear became a means of social control by religious and political authority during this period, animals came to be associated with human punishment – both real and imagined (in the afterlife, for example). Spectacles of torture and death inflicted on humans by animals (dogs, horses and pigs) became a form of community entertainment performed in public spaces to set an example. Animals were also present in the travelling circus, left over from the large spectacles of Roman times. Animals evoked nostalgia as their performances, which once dominated the metropolises, were relegated to the countryside. Most significantly, in the context of this book, animal-related spectacles during this period were at the intersection of performance events and daily life. Public executions, acts of shaming and punishment, animal baiting (carried out to soften the meat before its consumption) and staged hunts were all performed for both functional and entertainment purposes. Present in all of them, the animal enabled the crossing of boundaries, as these rituals fulfilled the practical and spiritual needs of the community.

Influenced by medieval bestiaries (biblical and animal stories written in Latin, which were very popular during the Middle Ages), medieval theatre performances typically employed animals as symbols, as allegorical subjects or as examples of human transformation. These associations, often divine or evil, continued into Renaissance and Elizabethan theatre traditions. In her article 'The Eight Animals in Shakespeare; or, Before the Human' (2009), Laurie Shannon points to the significant presence that animals had in early modern day-to-day life. Animals populated cities and towns, paintings, written texts, idioms and all sorts of popular entertainment, to the extent that 'Early Modern humans had more contact with animals than most of us do now' (p. 472). After medieval times, live animals all but vanished from the stage. This disappearance can be linked to the increasing professionalisation of the theatre from the sixteenth century onwards. In fact, it was not until the neo-avant-garde movements of the 1970s that animals reappeared onstage, as a way of challenging the border between reality and artifice. Although animals recurred in the works of Ben Jonson and Shakespeare, among others, and appeared in their plays' *dramatis animalia*, until the 1970s their live presence inhabited different locations: the baiting pit, the battlefield, the freak show and the circus.

In his introduction to *Stage, Stake, and Scaffold* (2011), Andreas Höfele suggests that these 'different' locations and the theatre might not, in fact, have been so far apart. Bear baiting contests and other staged animal fights were part of the cultural context in which theatre was written and produced, and were part of the everyday life of playwrights, actors and theatre managers:

> The culture that set the stage for Juliet and her Romeo, for a Falstaff and a Rosalind, also maintained a theatre nearby where animals could be watched tearing each other to pieces. Notable enough in itself, the truly remarkable thing about this is how much more it was than just coexistence. Play-acting and bear baiting were joined in active collusion. Vying for the attention

> of the same spectators, they were playing not just
> side by side or competitively against each other,
> but also, in the literal sense of Latin *colludere*,
> together. (Introduction, ebook)

Renaissance London, populated with numerous playhouses, was also the site of the first permanent baiting arena, where spectators paid to see fights between dogs, bears and lions. The coexistence, and indeed proximity, of the practices of theatre and animal baiting was, in Höfele's view, responsible for 'Shakespeare's explorations into the construction and workings of "the human" as a psychological, ethical and political category' (ibid.) and therefore contributed to the reflection on human–animal relations during the period.

As we enter the Enlightenment, animal-related spectacles began to be seen as insights into natural history, in accordance with the period's fixation on knowledge and its transfer. Kalof explains how the menageries, curiosity cabinets and exotic animal installations that were once restricted to the enjoyment of aristocrats were opened to the general public to provide the lower classes with an opportunity to learn about different species (p. 119). Although this gesture should be understood as a social act by the upper classes, it is yet another way in which animals, in this case exotic ones, have been used as accessories to display class differences in the public sphere.

It was also in the 1700s that the growing popularity of spectacles of animal-related cruelty produced an array of oppositional responses. And, although some of these practices were still being carried out at the beginning of the nineteenth century in the West, they had firmly disappeared towards its end. The increasing opposition to cruelty, and especially to its public demonstration, led to the birth of animal protection societies. The Society for the Prevention of Cruelty to Animals, for example, was founded in the United Kingdom in 1824. In turn, this led to new laws against cruel sports and the inhumane treatment of animals for entertainment. Thus, as ethical considerations became dominant and some practices were banned for their perceived cruelty, animals slowly disappeared from many performance contexts. The passing of time has had an interesting effect on public perception of certain traditions, as some practices that were deemed necessary in the nineteenth century (e.g. fox hunting) have become spectacles today, even when the people involved make utilitarian claims for their continued necessity. The utilitarian/non-utilitarian distinction has marked the ethical debate regarding the use of animals in performance contexts throughout the twentieth and twenty-first centuries, as demonstrated by the ongoing deliberations around practices which combine practical and spectacular motivations, such as fox hunting, bullfighting and rodeos.

The rise in moral and ethical concerns regarding animals that occurred during the nineteenth century, and that has continued throughout the twentieth and twenty-first centuries, was also linked to class. Some events that involved cruelty to animals were banned, as Kalof suggests, for their brutality and their association with the working classes. For example, while working-class practices such as animal baiting and animal fights were generally banned in England, those associated with the middle and upper classes, such as fox hunting, fishing and shooting, 'survived unscathed' (p. 136).

The locations in which animals were kept during the nineteenth century primarily enabled their display for humans or reinforced the dominion of culture over nature. Examples of this can be found in the popularity of stuffed animal exhibits in museums, in which animals were shown within recreations of their natural environment and performing their rituals in complex dioramas (for example, in the works of the American Carl Akeley and the English Walter Potter), and, of course, the increasing popularity of zoos.

For John Berger the nineteenth century was the time when humans and animals – for better or worse – parted ways. In 'Why Look at Animals?', the opening chapter of his book *About Looking* (1980), he explains that this was when 'every tradition which [had] previously mediated between man and nature was broken' (p. 3). As cities grew and societies became increasingly mechanised, animals were displaced by machines and relegated to spaces where, as rarities, humans could look at them. Zoos became extremely popular during this period, Berger argues, because they embodied colonialism and 'the capturing of the animals was a symbolic representation of the conquest of all distant exotic lands' (p. 21). As animals were framed in their cages, the zoo became a museum in which animals were looked at like art pieces.

The physical and cultural marginalisation whose origins Berger locates in the nineteenth century continues today. As animals have largely disappeared from the daily lives of humans, they have begun to appear in other locations. Performance becomes yet another venue for animals to be visible and for humans to continue to interact with, and reflect on, them.

This brief history of animals in theatre and performance contexts shows that animals have been primarily an object for human entertainment. From wild caged animals to tame trained ones, they have been utilised by humans to perform spectacular tricks – such as juggling, tight rope walking, following commands and performing cognitive achievements such as adding up and communicating with their human trainers – to mimic human behaviours or to participate in human-centred activities that have, in turn, become public displays of human dominion over the natural world.

Many of the practices described above have continued to be performed in the twentieth and twenty-first centuries. However, since the mid-twentieth century, owing to developments around animal welfare and a more critical engagement with human–animal relations, the presence of animals in theatre and performance has come to be strongly regulated by protection, health-and-safety and labour laws, in ways that have had an effect on how, where and when animals are used. The growing field of animal studies has equally shaped their use and representation in performance contexts as the writings of philosophers and critics have permeated the work of artists and theatre practitioners. Zoos, circuses, rodeos, hunts and similar contexts are still, in the twenty-first century, an embodiment of human control over the natural world. But philosophical debates around human subjectivity and alterity and, crucially, ideas around closeness, empathy and sharing between humans and animals have led many practitioners to work with, and alongside, animals in ways that seek to defy and challenge the traditional human–animal divide.

The following pages investigate animal presence and representation in relation to questions around the human–animal divide, ethics and the material conditions of performance. While this book looks mainly at contemporary practices, it does so with this historical introduction as its background, acknowledging the histories of animal performance and the questions that it has raised for centuries.

Animals, philosophy and ecology

Some of the major Western thinkers have attempted to engage critically with the notion of human subjectivity. And in their explorations of what it means to be human they have turned to the animal. Their ideas provide the framework for the deliberations in the following paragraphs. From Aristotle in the fourth century BC to Derrida in the twentieth, the question of what it means to be human has been tackled in terms of, in Derrida's own words in *The Animal That Therefore I Am*, 'the question of the animal', that is, the question of what it means not to be a non-human animal (p. 8). This question about the distinctiveness of species arises as a result of the inclusion, with the publication of

Charles Darwin's texts (*On the Origin of Species*, 1859; *The Descent of Man*, 1871; *The Expression of the Emotions in Man and Animals*, 1872) in the nineteenth century, of the human within the animal category. Until then, human thought had busied itself with demonstrating how animals were indeed different, and in most cases inferior, objects that existed to assist humankind in its development and progression.

To get a brief taster of these views, one can start by reading Aristotle's *Politics*. In Book 1, the philosopher expresses his belief that the human is 'the only animal who has the gift of speech', the only animal to have 'a sense of good and evil, of just and unjust', and, finally, the only 'political animal', which gives humans power over all other species (p. 13). In Aristotle's view, the lack of speech in animals also demonstrates their inability to reason, and thus their submission to their bodies. The Bible presents humanity in a similar position of superiority over animals. It is the first human, Adam – overseen by God – who gives animals their names. Derrida provides a close reading of the original scriptures in which this name-giving exercise is proven to grant the human absolute power over the animal world, which is from then on structured and ordered in human terms (pp. 15–18). This hierarchy informs how Western thought relates to, perceives and interacts with animals today, because, as Fudge points out in *Animal*, Christianity has naturalised anthropocentrism in the West (p. 14).

During the seventeenth century, European rationalism dominated Western thought. One of the central figures of this movement was the French philosopher René Descartes, whose views on the human–animal divide were highly controversial and are often still invoked in debates around human–animal relations and, above all, ethics. Descartes has been criticised for his description of animals as automatons that lack the capacity to feel and think. In his view, animals' actions could be explained purely by analysing their mechanical constitution. Cartesian thought is the origin of many contemporary views on animals' inability to think or feel empathy.

Philosophy's central position during the European Enlightenment brought questions about the nature of what it is to be human to the fore of social and political debates. The eighteenth-century German philosopher Immanuel Kant believed that 'willingness' distinguishes humans from animals. Willingness, in Kant's view, allows humans to control their actions and act in accordance with moral judgement. This capacity is lacking in animals, who are not able to control their desires. Their lack of control undermines their autonomy and makes them more dependent on others to make judgements. In Kant's conceptualisation, 'good will', the capacity to do good and to display moral judgement, provides a subject with intrinsic value. What follows, then, is that animals have no value, because they have no good will. Once again, the animal is a key agent in defining the human, and in maintaining the hierarchical dynamics that make humankind superior to other creatures.

The twentieth century was not a better one for animals. The key writings for the development of Western philosophy by Martin Heidegger and Emmanuel Lévinas lack serious attention to animals. Heidegger's seminal work, *Being and Time* (1927), is a reflection on the concept of 'being' from which beings other than humans are absent. The anthropocentric nature of this text manifests itself by omission and by, as Calarco suggests in *Zoographies* (pp. 15–54), the poor levels of engagement with animals found in some of the book's main arguments (e.g. on death). Lévinas' work on ethics is problematically anthropocentric too. For the French philosopher, the recognition of the other, which sets in motion an ethical response, is always predicated on a human other. Lévinas' ethics is based on the assumption that animals cannot be altruistic, that they cannot be concerned about the well-being of others. The reason for this, according to Lévinas, is that an ethical response requires that biological needs be suspended. Animals' failure to control their bodies means that they are incapable of caring for others. Calarco explains that for Lévinas, ethics is born out of the 'breaking with this biological order of being', and it is in the breaking that 'the human' arises (p. 56). It is the capacity for caring for the other that makes us human and distances us from the animal, which is driven by its biologically motivated animality.

Central to the progression of Western thought's understanding of the 'human', these views influence current human–animal relations and interactions and have contributed to the naturalisation of the notion of human supremacy over the natural world. Performance has also been shaped by these theories. The presence and treatment of animals in all sorts of human-led and human-consumed entertainment is regularly presumed and often uncontested. However, theatre and performance practices have also succeeded in creating a more productive platform for the investigation of human–animal relations, partly in response to those practices that have not, and partly influenced by the work of philosophers whose writings have challenged the centrality of the human.

In the twentieth and twenty-first centuries, there have been many influential voices whose intention was to expose the anthropocentrism of Western philosophy's metaphysical project. The works of Donna Haraway, Jacques Derrida, Giorgio Agamben, Gilles Deleuze and Félix Guattari, Peter Singer and Tom Regan are especially useful for understanding how performance has responded to this task. These authors have been instrumental in defining theatre and performance studies' engagement with 'the question of the animal', since their approaches have included performative elements or performance contexts: the gaze in Derrida, the concept of the 'anthropological machine' in Agamben, the idea of transformation and contagion in Deleuze and Guattari's concept of 'Becoming-Animal' (one of the various 'Becomings' suggested by the philosophers) and a conceptualisation of training in Haraway's work. Singer's and Regan's foundational contributions to the animal rights debate are essential to understanding the participation of animals in performance and have inspired the work of practitioners such as Rachel Rosenthal. Their views and conceptualisations will be fleshed out as the book progresses.

In the context of performance practice, the works of these philosophers prove particularly fruitful in three ways: understanding certain contemporary practices, some of which are a direct response to their ideas or texts; framing performance studies' engagement with the animal; and challenging established practices in which the animal's presence and participation is taken as a given.

Companion performers and bio-art: humans and animals share the stage

In her article 'Animals Love Theatre' (2007), Rachel Rosenthal expresses her unease around the presence of animals in performance: 'I have rarely been aware of artists using animals in a way that was respectful and humane. ... Placing them in an "art" context didn't hide the playing out of age-old attitudes vis-à-vis animals and our need to control and often hurt and kill, them' (p. 5).

Rosenthal, whose long career in the theatre has attempted precisely to counteract this problematic, believes that animals have been used in performance to fulfil one of two purposes: they have either represented 'humanity's callousness toward and dominance over other species' or they have been 'anthropomorphized and made to embody and represent human foibles or defects' (p. 5). Humans have demonstrated their dominion over other species in performances featuring animals – live, stuffed, trained, wild – such as learned pig shows, which featured a pig trained to follow commands in such a way that it appeared to solve mathematical equations or spell out words, wild animal circus acts, equestrian and water performances, and animal menageries, in which the animal follows the commands of the human and is praised for having acquired human-like skills (the most important of which is acting on cue). Animals such as Edward Albee's Sylvia, the goat in *The Goat, or Who Is Sylvia?* (John Golden Theatre, New York, 2002), or Michael Morpurgo's Joey, the main horse in *War Horse* (Royal National Theatre, London, 2007), serve a double purpose. On the one hand, they are human inventions used to explore certain traits of human subjectivity; they symbolise our concerns, our worries and our desires. On the other, given their existence within the context of the theatre, they are devices that both question and contribute to the performance's representational strategies.

Rosenthal's seemingly simplistic categorisation turns out to be accurate when we investigate the role of animals in human cultural history in general and performance in particular. However, one of the concerns of this book is to determine whether performance can overcome this solidified pattern and become a platform which allows human–animal interactions to be explored differently. In this section, I am interested in performance as a productive space to reflect on human and animal subjectivity, what it means to be human and to be animal, and how these two categories — as well as those of humanity and animality — continuously redefine each other.

Contemporary practitioners working on and with animals include Kira O'Reilly (United Kingdom), Catherine Bell (Australia), Orlan and Bartabas (France), and Rachel

Rosenthal and Kathy High (United States). In some cases, their practice explicitly responds to or engages with the writings of the philosophers mentioned above; in others, the philosophical writings help to illuminate certain aspects of their work. Overall, their work demonstrates that performance is a productive space in which to engage with debates around the human–animal divide.

Concerns about human–animal subjectivity, identity and hybridity are at the core of O'Reilly's and Bell's work. With a focus on the female body, the two performance artists have often interrogated human–animal relations in an attempt to blur the boundaries between the human body and the animal body. For instance, O'Reilly's *Inthewrongplaceness* (Penzance Town Centre, Penzance, 2006) and Bell's *Head over Eels* (Bellas Gallery, Brisbane, 1997) can be read as practical explorations of Derrida's concept of 'limitrophy', the subject of his 2008 book. The philosopher's attempt is to study the limit between human and animal, not to question whether there is any such limit (significantly, Derrida believes in a discontinuity between these two subjects). His aim is to determine 'the number, form, sense or structure, the foliated consistency, of this abyssal limit, these edges, this plural and repeatedly folded frontier' (p. 30).

O'Reilly's and Bell's performances interrogate this frontier by exposing the close proximity of these animal – human and non-human – bodies. *Inthewrongplaceness* features O'Reilly's naked body performing a series of movements with a recently slaughtered pig. During the performance, the two intertwined bodies become one, and their closeness to the spectator is an invitation to witness – and an explicit invitation to touch – this live symbiosis. The encounter is effective in inciting a reflection on our closeness to the animal whose flesh is one of the most consumed meats around the world and with whom face-to-face relations such as that featured in O'Reilly's performance are – in twenty-first-century Western cultures – scarce.

As Helen Cole points out in her review of the show in the journal *Antennae* (2010): 'Kira's limbs were entwined with the dead pig's, and because their skin colour was so close it wasn't immediately obvious which ones were hers' (p. 87). The performance is also effective in pointing to the closeness between pigs and humans, which recent science has suggested is both genetic (put into practice in pig-to-human organ transplants) and behavioural (demonstrated in studies of the causes of depression in humans and pigs). Jennifer Parker-Starbuck explains in her article 'Pig Bodies and Vegetative States' (2008) that O'Reilly's project is a bio-art one in which the artist's intention is to merge her own cells with those of the pig through a process of mixing biopsies. O'Reilly understands this as a process of getting to know 'oneself' in relation to one's boundaries:

> I am beside myself.
> How can I write about the body and bio art and
> a shuttling of desire to extend 'oneself' through
> the process of biopsy, cell isolation and cultiva-
> tion, through an appropriation and elaboration
> of a technology, and then to lose sight of oneself

because that extended presence cannot be considered any more 'one's self'. (quoted in Parker-Starbuck, p. 144)

Ideas around the human body's limits and its contamination with other bodies (including those of other species) have been a concern for O'Reilly in other works. In *Bureau of Decayed Visions/collective DNA extraction* (International Performance Art Festival, Warehouse 9, Copenhagen, 2009), for example, members of the audience donated DNA which was then mixed in a tube and inserted into her vagina, and *Finger Webs* (2009) is an online collection of images and videos featuring the building of spider webs between her fingers.

Bells' performance *Head over Eels* is a similar invitation to decentralise the human and to place human and animal bodies in a space that dilutes their boundaries. Dressed in a tight latex and neoprene suit that covers her from head to toe, Bell submerges herself in a pool filled with eels. Bell's body is lost in the blackness of the pool, its humanness transformed into a wet and slimy hybrid by proximity to the animals that outnumber and engulf her. This is, like *Inthewrongplaceness*, an improbable encounter. While eels are marketed and consumed as food, human interaction with them typically does not go beyond eating them or keeping them as pets. Bell's performance invokes hybridity as a way of understanding the human and the animal. She can barely be distinguished among the eels, as the performance places her body and the eels' bodies in a continuum of matter. In doing this, the performance, like O'Reilly's, reflects on the rigidity of the terms 'humanity' and 'animality' by bending the boundaries between these categories.

Film director and performance artist Kathy High, whose film *Lily Does Derrida: A Dog's Video Essay* (2010) is a direct response to Derrida's 2008 text, has devoted much of her performance work to investigating the human–animal distinction. Her ongoing project *Embracing Animal*, which produced a series of performance/exhibitions during 2004–2006, is an experiment to rescue and prolong the lives of three transgenic rats and to introduce the spectator to scientific experimentation on animals. High explains, 'I bought them to try and make them live as long as possible and to see if they could become healthy given their prior genetic conditioning' (*Embracing Animal* webpage). *Embracing Animal*'s performance/installation at the Massachusetts Museum of Contemporary Art in 2005 featured the three rats in the post-lab habitat that High created for them, which was designed to enhance human–animal interaction through the gaze. As the rats move freely through their space – a series of clear tubes, ramps and see-through enclosures – the spectator is encouraged to face the animal and grapple with the paradoxical relationship that he or she has established with it as pest or saviour of human lives: 'They are on exhibit here to introduce them and this research to you, the public. This special laboratory has been developed to extend their observation of humans and to extend their lives' (ibid.). High's flagging of the bi-directionality of the gaze in this encounter (the human and the animal are both observed observers) potentially begins a reflection in which the human has to come to terms with the hierarchical relationship built with rats in particular and animals in general.

O'Reilly's, Bell's and High's performances can also be understood as 'Becomings', an influential concept developed by Deleuze and Guattari in their co-authored volume *A Thousand Plateaus* (1987). The philosophers provide an opportunity to consider the gap between the human and the animal by both pointing to it and reassessing it. In considering this distance, the human engages in a process of 'Becoming' and defines himself or herself in relation to 'modes of expansion, propagation, occupation, contagion, peopling' (p. 239). In Deleuze and Guattari's view, animals and humans are not fixed categories but processes, 'Becom-*ings*', in which boundaries are an opportunity for openings and mergings. These processes don't happen through words – saying humans are animals is no longer enough. They take place at the level of cells and affect, as Deleuze and Guattari explain using the example of Hugo von Hofmannsthal observing the death of a rat:

> It is a composition of speeds and affects involving
> entirely different individuals, a symbiosis … . The
> rat and the man are in no way the same thing,
> but Being expresses them both in a language that
> is no longer that of words, in a matter that is no
> longer that of forms, in an affectability that is no
> longer that of subjects. (p. 258)

For the philosophers, 'the rat' and 'the man' are categories defined by language. Language is what divides them and separates them. However, the act of 'Being' is shared, and it is only outside the world of language, forms and categories that these divisions can be overcome. Kathy High's transgenic rats are a response to these ideas of expansion in which individual categories are challenged by transpositions, exchanges and 'Becomings' which contest established definitions of the human and the animal. In other bio-art experiments, including those performed by O'Reilly, human and animal forms are merged physically and affectively, forcing the human to reflect on what species are and what they mean in relation to the possibilities of assimilating and expanding with and into other species. For example, Orlan's *Harlequin's Coat* is a Plexiglas coat filled with cells from different origins, including the artist and a cow.

Far from the experiments of bio-art, French director and horse trainer Bartabas is interested in the possibility of building a relationship with the animal through performing. With his troupe Zingaro, he has been creating equestrian shows for more than thirty years. The director's journey towards this multispecies encounter begins with a disregard for the boundary between art and life. He explains that his exploration of human–animal relations goes beyond performance and insists that for him this is a way of life. He works and lives with horses on the outskirts of Paris at the Fort d'Aubervilliers, which also features a wooden theatre, their usual performance space. Zingaro's performances defy categorisation. They combine elements from the circus, dressage, poetry and music, with humans and horses at the centre. Sometimes they feature other animals. Bartabas defines Zingaro as a dance company of which horses are an integral part. Similarly, he frames his performances as a dialogue between man and animal. The man does not impose his will on the animal – although it could be argued that this is in fact done by using the animal to perform in the first place – but rather makes a proposition, resulting in performances co-created by man and horse. In an interview with Judith Mackrell for *The Guardian* newspaper in February 2011 he explains, 'In competition dressage, you have to have the horse completely under control. You have to go precisely from this step to this step. In my technique, I like the horse to be able to do the movement in his way. It's a very subtle thing, to do with his energy.' Having lived and worked with horses for years, Bartabas claims to build trust between animal and human performers. As he declares in an 'Inside Dance' interview for the opening of his piece *Le Centaure et l'animal* (2010) at London's Sadler's Wells, his work attempts to explain 'the relations between man and horse, and between men themselves, because the way you are with horses is the way you are with others'.

In *Le Centaure et l'animal*, Bartabas' mythical investigation into what it means to be human and to be animal crystallised in a collaboration between him, four horses and Butoh dancer Ko Murobushi. The show's intention is to erase the boundaries between man and animal, as Murobushi's almost naked body – in full silver makeup – contorts, starts and shakes, defying the limits of the human body, and Bartabas' horses perform with calmness and precision. At one point in the performance, man and horse appear to merge, and chiaroscuro allows the horse's head to become the man's and the man's body to become the horse's. This is the centaur – 'neither a man nor a horse, but someone between the two' – Bartabas explains in the 'Inside Dance' interview. The spectator is left to wonder who the animal of the piece's title is, as the only other body onstage is that of Murobushi.

Le Centaure et l'animal engages with an experience that, as Una Chaudhuri suggests in her article '(De)Facing the Animals' (2007), 'animal studies and animal art invoke compulsively': 'the animal as the Other to be faced' (p. 12). Introducing the centaur both as an embodiment of human–animal interactions and as a challenge to the human–animal divide, the show engages with the erasing of categories proposed by Deleuze and Guattari. This is a hybrid being, an unfamiliar face on a familiar body, a being that questions categories previously thought to be fixed. *Le Centaure et l'animal* aims to open up a mythical space in which animal and human are one but also separate entities, inviting the spectator to reconsider these limits.

Bartabas' life and artistic relationship with his horses is redolent of Donna Haraway's bio-philosophical writings on companion species. Haraway uses the metaphor of the 'cyborg' (a cybernetic organism, a hybrid made of biological and technological parts) to challenge feminism and identity theory in her text 'The Cyborg Manifesto', which was published in *Socialist Review* in 1985 and later as part of her book *Simians, Cyborgs, and Women* (1991). This hybrid identity allows Haraway to destabilise other established and socially constructed divisions such as nature–culture and human–animal. Her understanding of human–animal relations starts from the premise that 'we have never been human', as the human and other bodies are made of a variety of particles, cells and other organisms. In her book *When Species Meet* (2008), Haraway narrates the human–animal encounter in positive terms:

> I love the fact that human genomes can be found in only about 10 percent of all the cells that occupy the mundane space I call my body; the other 90 percent of the cells are filled with genomes of bacteria, fungi, protists, and such … I am vastly outnumbered by my tiny companions. (p. 3)

'Companionship' is a term that Haraway arrives at through her experience of co-performing with her dog, Cayenne Pepper, in agility shows. It is through companionship, and through the elements of performance-play, transformation, spectating, and training, that Haraway and Cayenne Pepper are able to 'meet'. The meeting, as she explains in *When Species Meet*, is an encounter of 'partners in the making' in which 'dogs and people learn to pay attention to each other in a way that changes who and what they become together' (p. 209).

Once again, performance and performance vocabularies are at the centre of the human–animal encounter, which they are instrumental in facilitating. Derrida's reflections on animals are prompted by a situation that resembles a theatrical experience: as he comes out of the shower, he finds himself being looked at by his cat. Spectating, the cat begins a process of reflection in the human; the meeting of their gazes initiates the encounter. Deleuze and Guattari's 'Becomings' are similarly theatrical. 'Becomings' are performative in that they both transform and require a transformation. Theatre (the performance space) as a place to see and to be seen, and performance's performativity, its transformational capacity, are essential to the staging of human–animal relations as understood by Haraway, Derrida, and Deleuze and Guattari. It is not surprising that performance practice has engaged with the question of the animal, and, indeed, that the question of the animal is raised by performance's workings. Theatre and performance practitioners and animal studies scholars have certainly used performance, its vocabularies and its methodologies to reconsider these relationships. However, as I explain in the following section, performance (especially with real animals) has to grapple with a history of animal subjugation to the human, and I wonder whether the 'Becomings' explained in this section produce a way in which this historical imbalance can be addressed.

Towards an ethics of animals in performance

The following pages examine animal performance from an ethical perspective. To this end, I propose that we expand Lévinas' concept of ethics, understood by Calarco in *Zoographies* as the act of 'being called into question by the face of the other' (p. 5), and consider that 'the other' can also be a non-human other. In my view, ethical considerations in relation to animals in performance demand an examination not only of how animals are treated and represented, but also of how the field of theatre and performance studies has looked at animal presence.

In *The Animal That Therefore I Am*, Derrida sets out to challenge what he perceives to be the West's 'immense disavowal' of the animal, which is at the heart of Western philosophy and symptomatic of human attitudes towards animals in general (p. 14). I start my exploration of the ethics of animal performance by looking at how theatre and performance studies have responded to Derrida's observations. Such scholars as Alan Read, Una Chaudhuri and Jennifer Parker-Starbuck have actively pursued a strand of research within this field that includes the animal, attempting to unmake the established assumption that the term 'performance' names an exclusively human-led and human-centred activity. Read's *Theatre, Intimacy and Engagement* (2009) tackles this assumption head on. In the second section of the book, entitled 'Performance as Such & on Human Performance in Particular', Read revives Walter Benjamin's term 'as such' to create a distinction between performance in general – 'performance as such' – and particular performances, in order to undermine a dynamic between these two concepts which has resulted in the particular being naturalised into the general (p. 82). In Read's view, this naturalisation has produced a situation in which one cannot think of performance as other than human, since most of the practices that performance studies scholars focus on are indeed human-specific. This assumption, Read explains, has led to statements which understand performance as a human-only venue, such as the following observation by Richard Schechner: 'Although a few species specialize in "deceit", most animal performances are automatically released, fixed and stereotyped' (quoted in Read, p. 107).

Later in the chapter, Read turns to Agamben's concept of the 'anthropological machine', which the philosopher explains in his text *The Open* (2004) as the mechanism by which humanity defines itself in opposition to the non-human. For Agamben, the anthropological machine 'functions by excluding as not (yet) human an already human being from itself... by animalizing the human, by isolating the nonhuman within the human' (p. 37). Read believes performance studies is an anthropological machine which 'works in affirming and resisting this separation between humans and other animals' (p. 82). As a solution to this problem he offers an understanding of life that is not associated with a particular species. This 'bare life', which Agamben describes as 'neither an animal nor a human life' (p. 37), is the life at the centre of performance practice in which all species participate.

These reconceptualisations would allow performance studies to engage with animal performance as other than mechanical – or as 'automatically released', in Schechner's Cartesian-infused terms (quoted in Read, p. 107). They would help us to understand the animal as a trained or trainable performer, but also as a subject that brings its own creativity to the performance. They would also offer an opportunity for the field to expand its remit and understand performance as other than human. As such, the presence of animals demands that practitioners, audiences, scholars and students alike reconsider their current approaches and methodologies; it demands a relocation of agency in which animals are not just objects in performance, but also its active agents.

Practitioners have attempted to address the disavowal identified by Derrida by integrating animals into performance in ways that undermine human sovereignty. In most cases, however, animals continue to represent the subjugated other who is trained to perform for the enjoyment and entertainment of humans. This means that performance practices have also played a part in Derrida's perceived disavowal by naturalising a well-established hierarchical paradigm. Some practitioners have attempted to address this problematic by working with animals beyond their use as mere objects. But the shadow of animals' (un)willingness to perform, as pointed out by Nicholas Ridout in his article 'Animal Labour in the Theatrical Economy' (2004, p. 58), also falls over the work of practitioners who believe themselves to be attentive to the needs and desires of animal performers. In my exploration of an ethical animal participation or inclusion in performance I do not want to conclude what is right or wrong, but rather to present the debates that have accompanied the presence of animals in performance for more than twenty years.

Does the animal want to be there? Agency and responsibility

I began this book with an instance of animal performance – Rodrigo García's rabbit scene in *After Sun* – which caused audiences to leave the theatre because they thought that what was taking place there was wrong. I now describe three more examples that might enable this discussion to work through performance's responsibility towards animals. The first of these is another piece by García, *Accidens* (Europeana Festival, Prato, Italy, 2005), which presented the live killing of a lobster that was subsequently cooked and eaten by a human actor. The second is animal mistreatment in circuses around the world, of which there are many accounts. Many circus animals undergo physical and psychological suffering; they are kept in inhumane conditions, chained, hit, poked, made to mate when they are too young and separated from their mothers at birth. Such practices are seen often in the West, despite the controversies and complaints that they raise; they are common in countries such as China, where, according to reports by Animal Asia, live animal performances that involve wire walking, jumping through burning hoops, standing upside down and boxing are still frequent. Ill-treatment, which affects elephants in particular, is invisible to uninformed audiences who attend these shows, despite the many public awareness campaigns, including those by PETA (People for the Ethical Treatment of Animals). Unlike in the case of *Accidens*, it is not part of the performance per se. The third example comprises the many animal performers on commercial stages in London and other cities around the world: the dog performers of hit musical *Legally Blonde* (Savoy Theatre, London, 2010), the cat in *Breakfast at Tiffany's* (Theatre Royal Haymarket, London, 2010), the real dog and fake lion in *The Wizard of Oz* (London Palladium, 2010) and the puppet pig in *Betty Blue Eyes* (Novello Theatre, London, 2010).

Human interactions with animals often spark ethical concerns. They have been closely monitored since the nineteenth-century foundation of animal protection agencies and the implementation of animal welfare laws (which differ from continent to continent). Animal welfare laws are regularly bent or broken in some of the planet's most secretive industries, and the treatment of animals by the food and pharmaceutical industries has repeatedly been a cause for concern among agencies such as PETA, the World Society for the Protection of Animals, the Humane Society and the Royal Society for the Prevention of Cruelty to Animals. In 1984, the first agency dedicated to the protection and rescue of performing animals was founded in the United States. PAWS (Performing Animal Welfare Society) monitors the use of animals in the entertainment industry and runs several sanctuaries where 'abused, abandoned and retired captive wildlife' live out the remainder of their lives. The existence of this – and other – dedicated agencies is perhaps an indication of the frequency with which animal welfare laws are broken in performance contexts.

Debates between animal rights and animal welfare activists – whose differences can be traced in the works of Tom Regan, Peter Singer and Robert Garner – have informed ethical approaches to the treatment of animals for decades. In a book co-edited with Cass R. Sunstein, *Animal Rights* (2004), Martha Nussbaum uses the phrase 'no cages or better cages' to summarise these two opposing approaches to the treatment of animals. The former approach advocates animal rights that prevent the use of animals by the food, pharmaceutical and entertainment industries; the latter agrees with the participation of animals in these industries provided their treatment is monitored and complies with the law. When we consider the presence of animals in entertainment, these debates prompt the fundamental question of whether live or represented animals should be there at all. In this section, I examine the presence of animals in performance, looking at the examples mentioned above and thinking through such concepts as anthropomorphism, representation and suffering.

Michael Peterson's article 'The Animal Apparatus' (2007) is a productive place to start thinking about the ethics of animal performance. For Peterson, the topic has too often been approached from an animal rights perspective. This means that the animals' experience of performing is considered from the point of view of our own – human – experience. Questions such as 'Is the animal suffering?' or 'Does it want to be there?' constitute a way of projecting human feelings and experiences onto animals, drawing on concepts such as sentience, agency and a shared vulnerability. They are also questions that rely on ethology, the study of animal behaviour. A more productive way of looking at animals in performance in relation to ethics, Peterson argues, is to read performances 'as constructions of social relations between humans and animals' (p. 34). In this way, an ethics of animal performance can begin differently than with questions such as whether animals should be there. Animals *are* there, whether we like it or not. So, in Peterson's view, we should look at what their presence says about how humans relate to them.

But can the spectator ever ignore the material conditions that surround the presence of real animals in performance? Does Peterson's approach mean that audiences should overlook how animals are treated and instead turn to how they – and our relations to them – are represented? In the case of García's *Accidens*, this would mean that the live killing of the lobster offered an opportunity to explore human concerns such as the assumption that animals are there to be killed and eaten, the disappearing act of 'killing to eat' (the show's appropriate sub-title) and the torture of a living being. Audiences should also, in this view, ignore the fact that the performance seems to be using the killing of an animal to reflect on the value of human life – an idea brought in by the projection of a series of texts around the fragility of human life in the context of a car crash while the lobster's killing is being performed. More importantly, perhaps, this approach would require the audience to turn a blind eye to the lobster's actual death. The interspecies performance featured in circus animal acts can also be read as a representation of social interactions between animals and humans. The animal's capacity to perform or its dexterity to perform certain sophisticated tricks is arguably a depiction of human control over animals (and the natural world in general). A reading in these terms, however, would result in our discounting how these animals are made to perform or what happens to them when they are not in the arena.

An ethical consideration of the participation of animals leads directly to the question of spectating. Does our participation in this experience – and, by being in the theatre, we are inevitably participating – imply an agreement with these relations? Do we have to leave the theatre, as did the spectators of *After Sun*, to end our contract with the ideologies that the performance is, knowingly or unknowingly, putting forward? This would certainly be Peter Singer's take on the matter. Singer's applied ethics follows on from the eighteenth-century philosopher Jeremy Bentham's utilitarian thoughts on animal rights. The result is an ethics driven by the concept of equality that is explained forcefully in Singer's most influential book, *Animal Liberation* (1990, 1995). For Singer, all species are equal, but not on equal terms: rather, they are equal on terms specific to each species (p. 5). The core of Singer's concept of equality is that 'the taking into account of the interests of the being, whatever those interests may be … must be extended to all beings, black or white, masculine or feminine, human or non-human' (p. 5). The needs that are to be taken into account are tailored to each individual subject, rather than to a group identified by race, gender or species. For its rights to be taken into consideration, a being has to be demonstrably able to suffer and to be happy: 'if a being suffers there can be no moral justification for refusing to take that suffering into consideration' (p. 8). So, do García's lobsters suffer? And, if we believe they do, is this suffering (and that of the millions of animals who take part in human-led performances every year) a reason to condemn the presence of live animals in performance? Following Singer, *Accidens* should be condemned for its 'species-ism' (a concept that the philosopher equates to racism and sexism both in its mechanics and in its outcomes), that is to say, 'a prejudice or attitude

44

of bias in favour of the interests of members or one's own species against those of members of other species' (p. 6). Both in the act that the performance contains (the killing and eating of a lobster) and in the social conventions in relation to animals that it represents (animals as food, animals as the property of humans, and so on), *Accidens* is an example of assumed human sovereignty over the natural world. In Singer's terms, the killing of the lobster is wrong, as it disregards the animal's right to live.

From this perspective, any performance that includes animals – whether or not they are killed – could be condemned on the grounds that the animals' needs are overlooked. Performances featuring live animals ignore the fact that the animals might not want to be there and, perhaps more crucially, the animals' right to live and not to suffer. Moreover, as Steve Baker suggests in '"You Kill Things to Look at Them"' (2006), the presence of animals in art can backfire. The animal body can, in some instances, be 'too much of an obstacle', an impediment to the spectator reflecting on the philosophical questions that the performance is grappling with (p. 72). The animal can prevent the performance from being able to move beyond the materiality of its presence. The shock produced by the killing of the lobster in *Accidens*, for example, means that the spectator cannot move beyond its death to think about what that death might mean.

David Foster Wallace's article 'Consider the Lobster', from *Consider the Lobster and Other Essays* (1995), introduces another useful concept relevant to performance contexts: 'preference'.

In his account of the annual Maine Lobster Festival, Wallace's reflections on the pain experienced by lobsters as they are cooked bring him to consider an ethics of eating animals. After navigating the various philosophical takes on sentience, Wallace concludes that the display of a preference by the animal is a prompt to reflect on how the animal is being treated:

> Still, after all the abstract intellection, there remain the facts of the frantically clanking lid, the pathetic clinging to the edge of the pot. Standing at the stove, it is hard to deny in any meaningful way that this is a living creature experiencing pain and wishing to avoid/escape a painful experience. To my lay mind, the lobster's behavior in the kettle appears to be the expression of a *preference*. (p. 251)

It is worth reflecting on animal performance in relation to this idea of preference. Their willingness or unwillingness to participate can be traced in the signs that animals display and the mechanisms that humans have had to resort to in order to counteract these signs. The performance space is a productive starting-point for these reflections. Animal performance frequently occurs in confined spaces in which the animal is contained, such as theatre buildings, arenas (circuses, rodeos, bullrings), cages (zoos, menageries) and water enclosures (aquariums, aqua parks). A large part of performing with animals is to make sure that they do not leave that space, to ensure, above all, that they remain visible to the audience. García's lobster is kept in a water tank before it is hung from a cable mid-stage; the dogs in Romeo Castellucci's *Inferno* (Barbican, London, 2010) are brought on to the stage on leashes by their carers and then chained to the stage's floor; the snake in Ivo van Hove's *Roman Tragedies* (Barbican, London, 2010) is carried by actors for the whole of its performance, and never left to move freely across the stage floor; the elephants, tigers and monkeys that star in circuses around the world are kept in cages, confined to the arena, or fed treats while performing, depending on the species to which they belong. The list is endless.

Feeding them treats is a commonly used tool to keep animals in the spotlight. Robert Wilson's *The Life and Death of Marina Abramović* (The Lowry, Manchester, 2011) opens with a group of Great Danes wandering around a stage filled with oversized fake bones. They occasionally disappear backstage, only to quickly re-enter. At first, spectators might wonder what is keeping the dogs onstage, what causes them to repeatedly return. They soon realise that the dogs are not freely wandering around, which is the illusion constructed by the performance, but are sniffing out the dog treats that, barely visible to the spectators' eyes, are also spread around the stage floor. The animals' attempts to leave the stage, and the fear that they will do so, demand that the performance put in place mechanisms that not only bend the animals' preferences, but also create a safe, controlled performance for both animals and humans.

The dozens of Chihuahuas and English bulldogs that have taken the parts of Bruiser and Rufus in the hit musical

Legally Blonde raise a different set of ethical questions. These animal actors embody yet another, potentially problematic, human–animal relationship. These animals are human creations whose habitats, needs and desires have also been designed by humans. As Erica Fudge explains in *Pets* (2008), pets are signifiers of an industry that, including food, toys, clothing and accessories, contributes £5 billion annually to the UK economy, with an average of £235 spent per animal per year (p. 3). In fact, UrbanPup.com – an Internet shop dedicated to fashion for dogs – is one of *Legally Blonde*'s producers, and a quick browse around the shop's web pages reveals a whole collection of pink attire under the banner 'Bruiser's Wardrobe. This much fun shouldn't be legal!'

Because of their status as pets it is difficult to judge these dogs' participation in performance in Singer's terms of suffering. These human-bred animals are used to cohabiting with humans; they are used to our environments and our interactions. However, they are still kept onstage by a constant supply of beef jerky, and made to perform tricks that humanise them, to the delight of audiences. Their anthropomorphised representation as dressed animals displaying human-like behaviours, resonant of the fake animals in Disney's *The Lion King, the Musical* (Orpheum Theatre, Minneapolis, 1997) and other Disney productions and products, certainly functions to maintain human sovereignty. The anthropomorphism is evidenced by the way they are described by Paul Taylor in his 2007 opening-night review for the *Independent* newspaper of the London Palladium production of *The Wizard of Oz* musical:

I found myself touched by the endlessly endearing Westmoreland terrier (one of four rotating in the role) who didn't put a paw wrong as Toto. With a quartet of canines here and eight in *Legally Blonde*, one wonders whether they all go off together for a post-show bowl of water at some Soho kennel and bitch about what a dog's life it is to be a four-legged star in the West End.

This flippant review is an example of what Chaudhuri, in '(De)Facing the Animal', calls 'the laugh test – that initial refusal to take the subject seriously at all' (p. 11). It is also an illustration of the inability to take animal performers into account and understand them in other than human terms. *Legally Blonde*'s objectification of the dogs, whose comedy acts are based on how well they can perform actions that humans find funny, contributes to the naturalisation of performance as a human-only activity in which animals are shaped for human entertainment.

It might seem that animal performance is inherently unethical, either because the animal has not agreed to participate or because its presence points towards a problematic representation of human–animal relations. Even Peterson's bid for a more constructive ethics of animal representation ends up deconstructing Bartabas' equestrian performances and demonstrating how intrinsically problematic they actually are. If Peterson's questioning of how animals are made to perform results in the complex dynamics of suffering, willingness and confinement explored above, his investigation of how animals are made to mean results in prescribed, exoticised, mystical and other troublesome understandings of issues such as 'wildness, nature, freedom, [and] servility' (p. 34). In his view, Bartabas' human–horse performances and his multispecies 'Becoming' discourse only offer the audience yet another 'eroticized fantasy of touching the other', a 'fantasy of a magical *human* transcending the species barrier' (p. 44).

Peterson's analysis means, crucially, that an assessment of the ethical questions that surround animal performance is relevant not only to the materiality of their participation (how animals are kept on- and offstage, how they are trained, transported, and so on), but also to their representation. Real animals do not actually have to be there to be mistreated or misrepresented. They can be there partially, as in the case of the part human/part animal costumes of *The Lion King* or *Cats* (New London Theatre, 1993); they can be there in puppet form, as in the latest animal stage hit, *War Horse* (New London Theatre, 2011); or they don't have to be there at all, as in the disappearing images of the elephant in Complicite and Tokyo's Setagaya Public Theatre's co-production *The Elephant Vanishes* (Barbican, London, 2003). There are real differences between live animal presence and other forms of animal representation, and the ethical questions raised by these two performance approaches need consideration. However, anthropomorphism is also at the centre of how non-live/unreal animals are represented. As human creations, either imagined or performing under complete human control, they are subject to humanity and its centrism.

Peter Singer's fundamental opposition to the mistreatment of animals has been influential for Rachel Rosenthal's animal performances. Her work, rooted firmly in the American avant-garde performance art tradition, shares approaches, content and methodologies with animal rights activism. *The Others* (Japan American Theatre, Los Angeles, 1985), for instance, is a direct response to Tom Regan's *The Case for Animal Rights* (1983) and Singer's *Animal Liberation*. The performance is an open manifesto for the animal rights cause. Opening with the Grimm's fairy tale *The Hut in the Forest*, in which a young girl is punished for overlooking animals' needs, and a direct attack on Descartes, *The Others* has a cast filled with human actors, and forty-two animals and their human companions. In the play, Rosenthal states that contemporary democracies are fascist regimes in which the lives of non-human sentient beings are oppressed: 'they are Other, and we are stronger, and we want to exploit their bodies and their minds' (p. 22). The performance intends to make a case for animal rights by shocking its audiences, and it does so by including several accounts of animal cruelty in a background projection featuring disturbing images of animal abuse on farms and in labs. It is hard not to be moved by the sheer number of animals that, as Rosenthal explains, are routinely killed by the food and pharmaceutical industries every year in the United States. But, however negative the performance presents human interactions with animals as being, her intention is also to demonstrate that 'otherness' can be a positive term that has the potential for inclusion. Rosenthal's performance is an attempt to challenge what she perceives to be an 'immoral use of animals in art' ('Animals Love Theatre', p. 5). And she proposes what she believes to be a more ethical way to include animals in performance. She does not ask the animals to perform tricks that embody human control over them or even to remain onstage: animals are 'left there to be themselves', free to move around and, crucially, free to leave (p. 5). She proposes instead an experience of performance that is a co-experience in which the animal is simply left to be itself as another being in the world.

Rosenthal's work is influenced by Haraway's understanding of 'companionship', as well as by her concept of 'otherness'. Together, these ideas are a helpful way to begin a positive engagement with animals in performance. Contained in *The Companion Species Manifesto* (2003), Haraway's ethics depart from an understanding of the other on its own merits, embracing its differences and its own characteristics. For Haraway, whose work focuses mainly on her relationship with her dog Cayenne Pepper, it is crucial to understand that 'dogs are not about oneself. ... They are not a projection, not the realization of an intention, nor the telos of anything. They are dogs; i.e., a species in obligatory, constitutive, historical, protean relationship with human beings' (pp. 11–12). To begin to formulate an ethics of human–animal interaction, Haraway believes that one has first to be aware of the animal as an individual. This awareness requires a degree of separation that enables the relationship to be productive rather than abusive. 'I believe that all ethical relating, within or between species, is knit from the silk-strong thread of ongoing alertness to the otherness-in-relation. We are not one, and being depends on getting on together' (p. 50). In Haraway's view, agility competitions embody a coming together of species through play. The process of training and performing with her dog gives Haraway the opportunity to rewrite the history of human–animal relations. In *When Species Meet*, Haraway describes how the experience of performing together in agility competitions provides her and Cayenne Pepper with a 'multispecies, subject-shaping encounter in a contact zone fraught with power, knowledge and technique, moral questions – and the chance for joint, cross-species invention that is simultaneously work and play' (p. 203). This is an encounter full of possibilities that, while still marked by the histories of abuse and control shared by woman and dog, also opens up a space for positive communication, interaction and learning. Their competitions lack the exoticism that underpins Bartabas' equestrian spectacles. They are not necessarily aimed at an audience; rather, they offer a common ground for the participants to communicate, learn, work and play with each other. However, the presence of animals in Rosenthal's work or in agility competitions is arguably always achieved by human imposition. I wonder what Rosenthal's more sensitive approach to animal performance does to the fact that the animals are still being put there by a human and how that addresses Singer's requirement to take into account the needs of the other. And I wonder whether Haraway's positive encounter owes something to our general perception of the dog as humans' best friend.

Finally in this section, performance's immediacy and its affectiveness have been productive in highlighting ethical questions around human–animal relations. These qualities have been central to the work of many artists who have found performance to be a direct, effective and wide-reaching way to engage in animal rights activism. A good example of this is the recent Fighting Animal Testing campaign initiated by the high-street brand Lush to call public attention to the ongoing delay to the passing of the EU *Cosmetics Directive* (a document that bans all animal experimentation in the cosmetics industry). The campaign included a ten-hour-long performance in April 2012 in Lush's Regent Street (London) shop window, where performance artist Jacqueline Traide underwent the experiments that animals are subjected to by the cosmetics industry, including force-feeding, eye-irritancy tests and saline injections. The Lush campaign relied on the transposition of human and animal bodies to get across its message against cruelty. Similar methodologies have been used by Theatre in Education companies to explore the topic of animal rights activism. The YMCA-based Y Touring Theatre Company, for instance, produced *Every Breath* (2006), a cross-curricular online learning resource debating animal experimentation.

Centuries of unequal human–animal relations in which the former has dominated, controlled and exploited the latter; the 'immense disavowal' of the animal by philosophy and the arts; and the visibility of animal welfare and animal rights movements have produced a situation in which any human–animal interaction necessitates ethical engagement.

As we have seen, performance is another venue in which the presence of the animal (live or not) initiates a process of questioning how this presence is ethically negotiated.

Risks, accidents and economics in animal performance

In his account of animals in Greek theatre, Arnott observes that live 'animals onstage are usually more trouble than they are worth' (p. 1). For the ancient Greeks, the presence of real, living creatures onstage necessitated expending a considerable amount of labour on the transportation, training and keeping of these animals. Health-and-safety regulations, an increasing preoccupation with risk, and labour and protection laws mean that, for contemporary practitioners, live animals are even more trouble. In sum, animals are difficult to control, they need to be trained, handled and constantly supervised, and they require care and attention before, during and after the performance.

While these concerns apply primarily to the participation of live animals, an engagement with the material conditions of performance is also required when decisions are made about using alternative, less difficult or less labour-intensive ways of representing animals. The use of animal puppets might have been a necessity rather than a choice in ancient Greece; according to Arnott, the Greeks often 'resorted to convention or impersonation rather than face the unrehearsed effects which would otherwise assuredly follow' if live animals were involved (p. 4). In contemporary theatre, having a puppet Joey for *War Horse* might be an aesthetic decision, but it also bypasses the health-and-safety regulations that would come with keeping the various horses required by the production in a central London location, and the risk involved in working with animals in live performance. However, many contemporary practitioners have stepped up to challenge 'the unrehearsed effects' that animals might produce, making that challenge a virtue of what animals bring to live performance.

Socìetas Raffaello Sanzio have for some time used live animals in their work as a way of reconnecting the theatre with its ancient Greek origins. In 2009, their piece *Inferno* arrived in London with a cast that included a horse and seven German shepherds – the breed of dog used in Pina Bausch's *Carnations* (Sadler's Wells, London, 2005) to represent the police state. *Inferno*'s opening scene represented precisely the challenge to risk that live animals allow performance to participate in. The production begins with one of the company's directors, Romeo Castellucci, presenting himself to the audience putting on a suit of padded body armour. In the meantime, the seven German shepherds are walked onto the stage by their handlers. Three dogs are set free and run to attack Castellucci, who is brought to the floor by their sheer strength, while the other dogs, chained to the stage floor, bark loudly. *Inferno*'s hair-raising opening is clearly dependent on the fear, violence and risk that these potentially dangerous animals bring to the performance. The loud, anxious barking of the chained dogs increases the sense of the ferocity of the attack, and the body armour, the handlers and the chains that contain the dogs' capacity to harm Castellucci (and potentially the audience) remind the spectators of the important, but fragile, nature of safety. The production, in fact, capitalises on the unnerving awareness of what could follow if a dog got loose from its carer, disobeyed an order or attacked an unprotected part of Castellucci's body. While these accidents rarely occur, they do happen, and *Inferno* is aware of the thrill that this potentiality brings to the performance.

The control exercised by trainers over animals that is at the centre of wild animal acts – and, to different degrees, all performances that involve live animals – has become a public demonstration of humans' dominance over the natural world. In these acts, beauty and dexterity, and thus intelligence, are designed to surprise, while more perilous routines are intended to shock and frighten the spectator. The risk involved in these acts is an undeniable component of their attraction, as spectators are aware of the possibility of things going wrong. But, on occasion, accidents happen and human and non-human animals are injured or die as a result. Such dramatic episodes form the backdrop against which any performance including animals is received. The spectator's trust is challenged by the knowledge that animal attacks do take place, and this possibility further heightens his or her experience and the value of the human–animal encounter. Furthermore, these stories work towards framing the animal as potentially violent and, in the worse cases, deadly, a fact that defines the performance and thus the audience's engagement with it. Fear and danger are key aspects of animal performance, and as such they are constructed and rehearsed to have a specific effect on the audience.

Peterson's article 'The Animal Apparatus' opens with a reference to the tiger attack on Roy Horn, of animal trainer couple Siegfried and Roy. This is perhaps one of the best-known examples of things going wrong when humans perform with animals. The attack occurred during an act with a white tiger in the long-running show *Siegfried and Roy at the Mirage* (Las Vegas, 2003). According to news reports, the animal attacked Horn and dragged him offstage by his neck. Roy survived the assault, but he was critically injured. One of the most interesting aspects of this event was the audience reaction, as recounted on CNN's website shortly after the accident: the shock and horror of witnessing a live attack was accompanied by the disbelief that what they were watching might not be part of the performance: 'A lady ran past me, freaking out and it was then I sort of, in the back of my mind, thought now this isn't part of the show,' said David Strudwick.

According to PETA experts, there have been thirty-five dangerous incidents involving elephants in US circuses since the year 2000 ('Circuses', n.d.). These accidents have involved elephants running loose through the streets, crashing into buildings, attacking members of the public, and killing and injuring handlers. In 1992, an elephant performing in the Great American Circus had to be shot after charging out of the venue with five children on her back. In 1994, an African elephant performing in the Circus International in Honolulu killed her trainer, injured twelve spectators and was finally gunned down after running loose through the city's downtown streets. However, as experts in elephant behaviour, such as Raman Sukumar in his book *The Living Elephants* (2003), repeatedly assert, such violent acts rarely take place in the animal's natural habitat. Elephants are infrequently involved in fights that end in serious injury. They live in structured societies organised around a matri-arch, and generations of females stay together in families throughout their lives. Experts are confident that the vio-lent behaviour exhibited by some circus elephants stems from the environment in which they are kept.

Similar risks surround the performances of orcas in aqua parks around the world. In her study of US chain SeaWorld, *Spectacular Nature* (1997), Susan G. Davis calls attention to the fact that the fear and danger at the heart of these per-formances actually have little to do with the animals them-selves; rather, they are constructed by the performance and by the unnatural conditions in which the whales are kept. Davis notes that in the SeaWorld performances of Shamu – a 12,300-pound orca also known as Tilikum – the animal 'is often referred to as a killer whale, rarely as an orca'; 'this widely popular name christens it as deadly' (p. 214). Davis also recounts how 'members of the audience bring with them the memories of accidents and deaths' that have taken place in the park (p. 214) – most recently that of trainer Dawn Brancheau, who was killed when Tilikum dragged her by her ponytail and drowned her during a live perform-ance in front of hundreds of terrified spectators in 2010. The court case that followed ruled out a decision to end the orca's life because the behaviour that killed Brancheau could in fact constitute play.

Accidents and deaths, risk and danger are part and parcel of live animal performance. And while these are infrequent, they play a part in constructing the experience of consuming any performance featuring live animals. Aqua parks, circuses, bullfights and contemporary theatre and performance practice work hard to create an illusion of danger that the animal, given its uncontrollable nature, embodies perfectly. Interestingly, these constructions are absorbed by the performance apparatus in ways that make them invisible to the audience, while crucially shaping their experience of it. Peterson argues that the tiger that attacked Roy Horn in 2003 was *performing* danger (p. 33). The animal had been tamed to control its predator instincts but was, at the same time, trained to display them on cue. And it seems that when it attacked Roy, it was doing just that. In her book *Wild and Dangerous Performances*, Tait also points to the constructed nature of 'wildness' and danger in circus acts. She explains that 'like actors, animal performers contributed to the theatrical text of emotions so that these became associated with them. ... Thus, during the twentieth century, big cats performed either docility or ferocity' (p. 3). So, while animals are generally perceived to obey, they can also perform disobedience. However, the training, a key aspect of many animal performances, is invisible to the audience, who are invited to experience a multispecies performance in which man controls beast. In the case of SeaWorld performances, Davis notes how unpredictability, and indeed accidents, are the part of the show that audiences love most. As a result, she states, 'the circus theme of nonconformity is written into scripts, so that the audience sees the animals in performance appear to defy their trainers' (p. 190). In the audience's eyes this defiance is real, and this is the thrill that puts bums on seats, as SeaWorld trainer Bob LaPorta explains in Davis' book: 'If … they come down for the Shamu show, and there's nothing it is a disappointment. It's terrible, a negative for them. It's not a good experience. … the best part is *always* when something went wrong' (p. 191).

Equally invisible are the causes of animals acting violently off-script: their removal from their natural habitat, the conditions in which they are kept (the proximity to other species, the separation of members of the same family or of mothers from their offspring, the size of the cages and the impact of transportation) and the psychological effects that all of these factors may have on the animal and its behaviour. Tilikum, for instance, was captured in the Pacific in 1983 and had spent nearly thirty years in captivity when the accident happened. Television and newspapers reports around the world were keen to emphasise the brutality of the attack and Tilikum's aggressive nature, reminding us of the whale's involvement in two previous incidents that resulted in the death of two humans. Tilikum's actions, however, were utterly unexpected, and when asked to comment on the orca's attack, various whale experts have concurred on the danger of keeping these animals in captivity.

In my article 'Never Work with Children and Animals' (2010), I explore the ways in which contemporary performance practice involving children and animals represents an embodiment of and a challenge to contemporary society's obsession with risk. The live animal onstage poses a potential risk to the human, and vice versa, it can signify a challenge to risk-averse and risk-prone socio-politico-economic structures, and it can also embody these risks and fears. As issues of predictability, agency and intentionality are key to animal behaviour within performance contexts, the presence of live animals in performance can be simultaneously understood as a symptom and cause of, and a challenge to, the 'risk society', the influential concept originated by Ulrich Beck in *Risk Society* (1992) and expanded in *World at Risk* (2009). In Beck's view, risk is an element of political, social and economic control in contemporary societies in which the individual has become solely responsible for his or her own well-being and that of the planet. This is a process that Anthony Giddens, in his article 'Risk and Responsibility' (1999), calls 'responsibilization', in which the level of individual responsibility increases in a context of continuous uncertainty. As Giddens states, 'we don't know, and we can't know' (p. 9).

As I argue in my article, the risk-taking and responsibility that come with animal performance are 'more than just performance methodologies. They are also performance's engagement with the political, social, economic and cultural shifts that these processes continue to bring about' (p. 82). Animals generate an opportunity for performance to challenge these processes of risk-taking and responsibilisation by pushing the boundaries of what can, might or should happen onstage. Contemporary theatre practitioners associated with avant-garde and experimental practices, such as Socìetas Raffaello Sanzio (Italy), Jan Fabre (Belgium), Rodrigo García (Spain), Wim Vandekeybus (Belgium), Quarantine (United Kingdom), Les Ballets C de la B (Belgium), Àlex Rigola (Spain) and Pina Bausch (Germany), have used live animals in their work as a way of challenging the increasing regulation of artistic practice. Animals keep everyone on their toes: practitioners, audiences and regulators. And this unpredictability is a valuable currency in a market – that of experimental practice – driven by provocation and risk-taking.

In the theatre, health-and-safety regulations have come to embody political, social, economic and cultural constraints, and animals are a direct challenge to them. In the United Kingdom, for instance, the presence of animals in performance represents an automatic engagement with the law. Any human–animal relations are legislated by the *Animal Welfare Act 2006*. Interactions in performance contexts are regulated by the *Performing Animals (Regulation) Act, 1925*, which was amended slightly in 1968. The latter Act demands that any performing animal and its carer register with the local authority and acquire, upon the payment of a fee, a licence to perform. These laws and regulations provide the authorities with a means of controlling the use of live animals in performance. Interestingly enough, the Act does not apply 'to the training of animals for bona fide military, police, agricultural or sporting purposes, or the exhibition of any animals so trained' (Chapter 38, Clause 7). These exceptions to the application of the Act explain, *inter alia*, the legality of sports such as fox hunting in the United Kingdom. A more recent document which speaks to the increasing pre-occupation with safety was issued by the Health and Safety Executive in 2011: *Working with Animals in Entertainment*. It contains a series of recommendations for working safely with animals and is designed to protect and safeguard humans. It invokes general legislation in the United Kingdom regarding health and safety, proposes that expert risk assessments are carried out and lists a series of control measures whose aim is to minimise or eliminate risks from animals. It is evident from these documents, however, that the regulations regarding performing animals are culturally specific. The Western concern with policing should not be taken to be general: in other parts of the world, animal performance takes place in less regulated contexts.

Health-and-safety and risk-control policies are concerned with the well-being of animals but do not account for their participation in the theatre economy. While in many instances animals increase the value of a performance, their labour is unaccounted for. In his article 'Animal Labour in the Theatrical Economy', Ridout explores this issue in relation to the perceived exploitation that follow from the fact that animals do not participate fully in the economics of the theatre industry: they do not get paid, even for overtime, they are not represented by an agent and the number of hours they work is not regulated. For Ridout, their exploitation might bring them closer to their human co-performers, with whom they share a history of unfair labour conditions. However, their human counterparts get paid for their job, and we might wonder how animals benefit from participating in the theatre, and other entertainment industries.

The participation of live animals is also dictated by economics. Quarantine's *Old People, Children and Animals* (Contact Theatre, Manchester, 2008) brought together a cast of human performers, a group of rabbits and a parrot. The parrot opens the performance, but at £250 a day, the parrot is an expensive performer and its price limits the number of hours that the company can work with it. The cost of animal performers – hiring, transportation, handlers and trainers – is balanced against the financial benefits that they might produce and, going back to Arnott, the nuisance that they might generate. Meanwhile, centuries of human–animal interactions have naturalised their presence in ways that make invisible the extent to which animals shape how performance happens. The policing of their presence and the costs that they impose on productions are yet another proof of how much they matter.

Animals and their representations in performance

In *Coyote: I Like America and America Likes Me* (1974), German artist Joseph Beuys delivered himself as a package – carried from the airport wrapped in a felt bundle – to the New York gallery that was to stage his seven-day performance. Once he had been deposited in the enclosure where the performance was to take place, it was down to Little John, the live coyote that accompanied Beuys in this venture, to unwrap the artist. Beuys and Little John's interactions were, at first, a series of ritualised actions and games, but as Steve Baker points out in his chapter in Cary Wolfe's *Zoontologies*, 'Sloughing the Human' (2003), the performance became 'a mainly improvised encounter as the week progressed' (p. 149). Spectators attending the performance would have wondered about the meaning of this encounter and Little John's signification within it. David Williams suggests in his examination of the performance in 'Inappropriate/d Others' (2007) that 'in the mythical narrative of loss and return that Beuys ... purported to enact here, the coyote was a stand-in for the "wound" of America and the repressed knowledge of its indigenous people' (p. 99). However, as Williams goes on to argue and Baker suggests in *The Postmodern Animal* (2000, p. 80), the animal has no fixed meaning: in art practice 'animals signify too much'.

Little John is made to mean by Beuys' piece, but it also carries its own culturally constructed meanings – ferocity, cunning, freedom, wildness – which feed into the performance's meaning-making processes. Paradoxically, however, as a real animal in a performance context, it also resists being completely assimilated into these processes. Little John is simultaneously a coyote, a sign and a desire. The coyote's refusal to be fixed explains the crucial role that animal presence has played in avant-garde and experimental art, given these practices' central preoccupation with the blurring of boundaries between artifice and reality. At the crossroads between the real, the imagined and the illusory, animals are well equipped to undertake this task.

The presence of animals in the work of neo-avant-garde and experimental theatre practitioners and performance artists in Europe, the United States and Asia is well documented in the articles included in Chaudhuri's special issue of *The Drama Review* (2007). When theatre wants to challenge its own theatricality, the animal enters the stage. Interestingly, animals are crucial to debates around the performance/theatre split, as explored in Stephen J. Bottoms' article 'The Efficacy/Effeminacy Braid' (2003). The attempts of a 'generation of experimental theatre makers to "ritualize" theatre by various means; to seek to make it more "efficacious" in the lives of its participants' that Bottoms refers to in his article meant the inclusion of ritual aspects in the theatre – and with the ritual, came the animals (pp. 174–75). This is why animals have been so prominent in experimental performance from the 1960s until today: their status destabilises the binary, which Bottoms sets out to challenge in his article, between 'authentic reality' and 'illusory representation' (p. 174).

Ridout's and Williams' writings suggest that animals in performance are neither only animals (real) nor mere signs (representations), despite the many instances of performance practice that treat them as precisely either of those things. In 'Animal Labour in the Theatrical Economy', Ridout challenges the idea that 'the animal on stage in contemporary theatre and performance is usually understood, and often ... deployed as an insistence upon an irreducible materiality' (p. 60). The fact that animals have been understood to have 'no meaning, no history' and no political standing has meant that, on the one hand, animals are a stand-in for the real and, on the other, they are an empty sign to be given signification (p. 60).

Animals are brought onto the stage specifically to break the system of representation that the theatre is concerned with. As Ridout suggests, the animal 'is not pretending or representing anything or anyone; it is what it is, and it does what it does, and it means nothing by it' (p. 60). An example of this can be found in Pan Pan's deconstruction of William Shakespeare's *Hamlet*, a text famously concerned with the power of theatricality, in *The Rehearsal: Playing the Dane* (Samuel Beckett Theatre, Dublin, 2010). Pan Pan expose the workings of *Hamlet* in different ways: the audience is made privy to how it is put together, rehearsed and, finally, performed. We sit through the auditions for the main role and production meetings, and see the play's main characters split into many bodies, including those of the audience. In the midst of all this, *The Rehearsal* also includes a real Great Dane who is brought onto the stage at various points in the performance. The dog embodies another way of undermining representation. It is simultaneously a personification – or, I should say, an animalisation – of Hamlet, the Dane, and a 'real' Great Dane, and, as such, it disrupts the illusion and exposes the constructedness of the theatre.

However, in his book *Stage Fright, Animals, and Other Theatrical Problems* (2006), Ridout wonders whether animal performance can really resist meaning-making. Once animals appear in a context where what is presented is also a representation of something else (and that is the context of the theatre), they are not just animals; they are part of the illusion that the performance creates. The animal's participation, Ridout explains, 'in the human activity of making a show automatically puts it in the place where that which is shown is also theorized (that place called the theatre) and where even the mouse in the house cannot evade the labour of meaning-production' (p. 102). Does this mean that, willingly or unwillingly, animals in performance will always be readable signs? In his analysis of animal presence – live/real and fake – in the work of Socìetas Raffaello Sanzio, Ridout seems to be suggesting just that ('Make Believe', 2006). In 'The Animal Being on Stage' (2000), the director Romeo Castellucci explains that in SRS's work, the animal encapsulates the origins of tragedy – etymologically 'the song of the goat': *tragos* (goat) and *aoidê/ôidê* (song) – which is born when the sacrificial animal disappears from the stage (p. 24). This means that animals exist before the moment of representation, before the birth of theatre. However, Ridout suggests that Castellucci's inclusion of animals to bring theatre back to a moment before representation may not in fact be as successful as the director believes. The presence of a real horse in the company's production of *Giulio Cesare* (Queen Elizabeth Hall, London, 1997) resists being assimilated into the performance's production of meaning because of its association with the environment in which it is presented (the theatre, the other animals onstage, the human performers, the other objects) and the treatment that the animal receives. Ridout concludes that 'because the "real, live" horse is dragged into the world of signs by this network of relations between meaningful bodies, it is, beyond question being used as a sign' (*Stage Fright*, p. 105).

And this is a role that animals regularly fulfil in performance practice: aiding practitioners in the production of meaning for audiences to interpret. In Mal Pelo's production *He visto caballos* ('I Have Seen Horses') (Mercat de les Flors, Barcelona, 2008), based on the writings of John Berger, the animals have a very specific meaning. The show focuses on two individuals (possibly a couple), performed by company dancers and directors Maria Muñoz and Pep Ramis, who are experiencing a period of crisis. Unable to communicate with one another, they are separately trapped in their own worlds. This separation is represented in scenes in which the performers dance on their own on the empty stage, and also in a section entitled 'Separation', when we see a long projection of a horse running free. At different points in the performance the same horse is projected in negative on the background, haunting the couple as they struggle to share the same space. The horse's meaning is offered in the narrative that accompanies the performance: 'The horses' images appear as a metaphor for freedom, which is the secret that these two individuals have to invent while they are apart.' *He visto caballos* constructs animality as a form of freedom in opposition to a humanity that is trapped in its own individuality and confusion. The horse, whose movements have also left a trace in the dance, is used to signify the freedom that might allow the human to escape from himself or herself. At one point in the performance, Muñoz makes this clear in a monologue accompanied with movement: 'Suddenly I started making mad gestures. Yes! I neighed like a horse, bent my mane backwards and stomped the floor. Celebrating a moment of freedom. Yes! Like a mad woman.'

A similar opposition between animality and humanity is displayed in Complicite and Setagaya Public Theatre's *The Elephant Vanishes*, in which the animal, in this case an elephant, is again used as a stand-in to understand humanity. The show is based on the blending of three texts from Haruki Murakami's collection of short stories of the same title, and it explores the subjugation of humanity to technology and the urban. The disappearance of an elephant from Tokyo's zoo is the starting-point of this metaphor. Fleeting images of the animal body are scattered across TV screens, newspaper photographs and screen projections. It seems as if nature can be accessed only through technology; the untouchable images of a deconstructed elephant are the remains of humanity's connection with the natural world. While the production incisively speaks to the disappearance of animals from our day-to-day urban and technology-populated lives, it also creates a mystical approach to nature: the animal signals a desire to repair an irreparable loss. *The Elephant Vanishes* explores the idea that the concept of humanity is no longer fixed owing to the relationships that the human has established with technology as well as with animals. The elephant in the production is displaced and becomes virtual; it is a real animal but also a metaphor for other things human: nostalgia for a non-technological world.

These examples of animal signification ensure the animals' readability in a world to which they do not belong. The place of representation that is the theatre cannot cope with what cannot be represented, and that is why live animals are rarely used as signs. This does not mean that all the other ways in which animals appear in performance (puppets, furries, images, sounds, movements) are always pointing towards a specific signification, as we have seen in the case of Mal Pelo or Complicite/Setagaya. These are animals that represent other animals. The various furries (chicks, frogs, rabbits, rats) that populate the stage in Jan Fabre's *Parrots and Guinea Pigs* (De Singel, Antwerp, 2002) are manmade versions of real animals, and that is exactly what they are intended to signify. They are there precisely to destabilise the multifarious ways in which animals are represented. Fabre's chaotic multispecies encounter wants to ask questions about what it means to be human and to be animal (as humans and animals share movements, nakedness, food, bodily functions). The production aims to interrogate how these two categories are represented in the theatre by presenting a stage on which human and animal bodies are confused with their own representations: the anthropomorphised figure of the furry. The show fights the human projection of meaning onto animals and presents, as Marvin Carlson suggests in his review for *The Drama Review*, 'the work of (in the most comprehensive and laudatory ways) "performing animals"' ('I Am Not an Animal', 2007, p. 169).

Simon McBurney's opera *A Dog's Heart* (English National Opera, London, 2010), based on the Mikhail Bulgakov novella *The Heart of a Dog* (1925), has, at its centre, a puppet dog designed to represent a real dog named Sharik. Puppetry is Complicite's way of dealing with the improbable transformation that *A Dog's Heart* requires – that of a dog who becomes a man. It also allows for the controlled performance of an uncontrollable animal. In a production that condemns human greed and ambition in relation to the practice of eugenics, the animal puppet – brought to life by the work of puppet theatre company Blind Summit – is yet another embodiment of human control. On the other hand, Sharik's fakeness allows for an intervention into theatre's representational strategies. Sharik's dismembered body, its constructed nature, movements and voice (split between two singers), point to the fact that what we are seeing is not real. Yet again the animal is both a sign and a device to expose performance's workings and meaning-making structures.

The aim of this book has been to demonstrate how animals intervene in how theatre and performance is produced, received and disseminated by challenging the established ways in which theatre and performance studies scholars and practitioners relate to their objects of study and practices. The examples of animal presence in performance included in this book – and many more that could not feature in it – and the increasing volume of scholarly work focusing on animals evidence a renewed interest in animals in performance contexts. As this book has shown, looking at animals in these contexts requires an engagement with other disciplines, which in turn means that animals facilitate performance's intersections with wider societal and intellectual concerns and debates.

further reading

There are no monographs dedicated to the presence of animals in theatre and performance contexts. This work is spread across articles in various journals, and chapters in books concern with other issues. Una Chaudhuri's and Alan Read's special issues of *The Drama Review* (2007) and *Performance Research* (2000), respectively, focused on theatre and performance practices with animals at their core. In addition, there have been single articles published in academic journals and monographs within the field, such as Nicholas Ridout's seminal articles 'Animal Labour in the Theatrical Economy' (2004) and 'Make Believe: Socìetas Raffaello Sanzio Do Theatre' (2006) and the section on animals included in his book *Stage Fright, Animals, and Other Theatrical Problems* (2006). Alan Read (*Theatre, Intimacy and Engagement: The Last Human Venue*, 2009), Jennifer Parker-Starbuck ('Becoming-Animate: On the Performed Limits of "Human"', 2006), Laurie Shannon ('The Eight Animals in

Shakespeare; or, Before the Human', 2009) and Marla Carlson ('Furry Cartography: Performing Species', 2011) have all questioned anthropocentric approaches to performance in their writings, challenging the centrality of the human in performance and Performance Studies, and offering insights into more hybrid – and more inclusive – understandings of practice and scholarship. The work of Peta Tait (*Wild and Dangerous Performances: Animals, Emotions, Circus*, 2012) and John Stokes ('"Lion Griefs": The Wild Animal Act as Theatre', 2004) on animal performance in the circus has been crucial in closing the gap between Theatre and Performance Studies and the interdisciplinary field of Animal Studies.

Romeo Castellucci, Kira O'Reilly, Kathy High and Rachel Rosenthal are some of the practitioners who have openly written about their work with animals. Their writings and websites are a useful resource to understand their interest in performing with other species.

Animals in performance contexts necessarily require an engagement with philosophy. In addition to reading the work of the philosophers themselves, Matthew Calarco's *Zoographies: The Question of the Animal from Heidegger to Derrida* (2008) is a useful book for understanding their complex texts. Similarly, Erica Fudge's *Animal* (2002) is a valuable resource to obtain a general knowledge base from which to explore other, more specific readings. Finally, Steve Baker's *The Postmodern Animal* (2000) is essential reading for understanding animal presence in postmodern art and performance practice. Finally, the Reaktion books series on animals with books dedicated to various animals, offers an excellent insight into animals and their role in science and cultural history.

Agamben, Giorgio. *The Open: Man and Animal*. Trans. Kevin Attell. Stanford, CA: Stanford UP, 2004.

Aristotle. *The Politics and The Constitution of Athens*. Ed. Stephen Everson. Cambridge: Cambridge UP, 2010.

Arnott, P. D. 'Animals in the Greek Theatre.' *Greece & Rome* 2nd ser. 6.2 (1959): 177–79.

Baker, Steve. *The Postmodern Animal*. London: Reaktion, 2000.

———. 'Sloughing the Human.' *Zoontologies: The Question of the Animal*. Ed. Cary Wolfe. Minneapolis: U of Minnesota P, 2003.

———. '"You Kill Things to Look at Them": Animal Death in Contemporary Art.' *Killing Animals*. Animal Studies Group. Urbana: Illinois UP, 2006. 69–99.

Bartabas. 'Inside Dance.' Interview. Sadler's Wells. <www.youtube.com/watch?v=yGTD7meQ4iE>. Accessed 12 April 2012.

Beck, Ulrich. *Risk Society: Towards a New Modernity*. Trans. Mark Ritter. London: Sage, 1992.

———. *World at Risk*. Cambridge: Polity, 2009.

Berger, John. 'Why Look at Animals?' *About Looking*. New York: Pantheon, 1980. 1–26.

Bottoms, Stephen J. 'The Efficacy/Effeminacy Braid: Unpicking the Performance Studies/Theatre Studies Dichotomy.' *Theatre Topics* 13.2 (2003): 173–87.

Calarco, Matthew. *Zoographies: The Question of the Animal from Heidegger to Derrida*. New York: Columbia UP, 2008.

Carlson, Marla. 'Furry Cartography: Performing Species.' *Theatre Journal* 62.2 (2011): 191–208.

Carlson, Marvin. '"I Am Not an Animal": Jan Fabre's Parrots and Guinea Pigs.' *The Drama Review* 51.1 (2007): 166–69.

Castellucci, Romeo. 'The Animal Being on Stage.' *Performance Research* 5.2 (2000): 23–28.

Chaudhuri, Una. 'Animal Geographies: Zoöesis and the Space of Modern Drama.' *Modern Drama* 46.4 (2003): 646–62.

———. '(De)Facing the Animals: Zooësis and Performance.' *The Drama Review* 51.1 (2007): 8–20.

——— ed. *Animals and Performance*. Spec. issue of *The Drama Review* 51.1 (2007).

Cole, Helen. 'Kira O'Reilly: *Inthewrongplaceness.*' *Antennae* 12 (2010): 87–91.

Davis, Susan G. *Spectacular Nature: Corporate Culture and the Sea World Experience*. Berkeley: U of California P, 1997.

Deleuze, Gilles, and Felix Guattari. '1730: Becoming-Intense, Becoming-Animal, Becoming-Imperceptible ...' *A Thousand Plateaus: Capitalism and Schizophrenia*. Minneapolis: U of Minnesota P, 1987. 232–309.

Derrida, Jacques. *The Animal That Therefore I Am*. Trans. David Wills. Ashland, OH: Fordham UP, 2008.

Every Breath. Judith Johnson. Y Touring Theatre Company, 2006. DVD. Trailers available at <www.theatreofdebate.com/Resources/ Resources/EveryBreath.html>. Accessed 2 June 2012.

Flynn, Clifton P. *Social Creatures: A Human and Animal Studies Reader*. New York: Lantern, 2008.

Fudge, Erica. *Animal*. London: Reaktion, 2002.

———. *Pets*. Stocksfield, UK: Acumen, 2008.

Giddens, Anthony. 'Risk and Responsibility.' *Modern Law Review* 62.1 (1999): 1–10.

Haraway, Donna J. *The Companion Species Manifesto: Dogs, People, and Significant Otherness*. Chicago, IL: Prickly Paradigm, 2003.

———. *When Species Meet*. Minneapolis: U of Minnesota P, 2008.

High, Kathy. 'Playing with Rats.' *Tactical Biopolitics: Art, Activism and Technoscience*. Ed. Beatriz da Costa and Kavita Philip. Cambridge, MA: MIT Press, 2008. 465–78.

Höfele, Andreas. *Stage, Stake, and Scaffold: Humans and Animals in Shakespeare's Theatre*. Oxford: Oxford UP, 2011.

Kalof, Linda. *Looking at Animals in Human History*. London: Reaktion, 2007.

Kluger, Jeffrey. 'Killer Whale Tragedy: What Made Tilikum Snap?' *Time* 26 February 2010. <www.time.com/time/health/ article/0,8599,1968249,00.html>. Accessed 10 March 2012.

Latour, Bruno, and Peter Weibel. *Making Things Public: Atmospheres of Democracy*. Cambridge, MA: MIT Press, 2005.

Lippit, Akira Mizuta. *Electric Animal: Toward a Rhetoric of Wildlife*. Minneapolis: U of Minnesota P, 2000.

Lonsdale, Steven. 'Attitudes towards Animals in Ancient Greece.' *Greece & Rome* 2nd ser. 26.2 (1979): 146–59.

Mackrell, Judith. 'Bartabas: Dances with Horses.' *Guardian* 21 February 2011. <www.guardian.co.uk/stage/2011/feb/21/bartabas-zingaro-dance-horses-interview>. Accessed 8 January 2013.

Marjanić, Suzana. 'The Zoostage as Another Ethical Misfiring: The Spectacle of the Animal Victim in the Name of Art.' *Performance Research* 15.2 (2010): 74–79.

Omond, Tamsin. 'Lush's Human Performance Art Was about Animal Cruelty Not Titillation.' *Guardian Online* 27 April 2012. <www.guardian.co.uk/commentisfree/2012/apr/27/lush-animal-cruelty-performance-art>. Accessed 2 June 2012.

O'Reilly, Kira. 'Bio Art.' <www.kiraoreilly.com/blog/archives/category/bioart>. Accessed 2 June 2012.

Orozco, Lourdes. 'Never Work with Children and Animals: Risk, Mistake and the Real in Performance.' *Performance Research* 15.2 (2010): 80–85.

Parker-Starbuck, Jennifer. 'Becoming-Animate: On the Performed Limits of "Human".' *Theatre Journal* 58.4 (2006): 649–68.

———. 'Pig Bodies and Vegetative States: Diagnosing the Symptoms of a Culture of Excess.' *Women and Performance: A Journal of Feminist Theory* 18.2 (2008): 133–51.

PETA. 'Circuses.' <www.peta.org/issues/animals-in-entertainment/circuses.aspx>. Accessed 18 March 2012.

Peterson, Michael. 'The Animal Apparatus: From a Theory of Animal Acting to an Ethics of Animal Acts.' *The Drama Review* 51.1 (2007): 33–48.

Read, Alan, ed. *On Animals*. Spec. issue of *Performance Research* 5.2 (2000).

———. *Theatre, Intimacy and Engagement: The Last Human Venue*. Basingstoke, UK: Palgrave Macmillan, 2009.

Ridout, Nicholas. 'Animal Labour in the Theatrical Economy.' *Theatre Research International* 29.1 (2004): 57–65.

————. 'Make Believe: Societas Raffaello Sanzio Do Theatre.'
Contemporary Theatres in Europe: A Critical Companion. Ed. Joe
Kelleher and Nicholas Ridout. London: Routledge, 2006. 175–87.

————. *Stage Fright, Animals, and Other Theatrical Problems*. Cambridge:
Cambridge UP, 2006.

Rosenthal, Rachel. 'Animals Love Theatre.' *The Drama Review* 51.1
(2007): 5–7.

————. *The Others*. Unpublished text. 1985.

Rothfels, Nigel. *Representing Animals*. Bloomington: Indiana UP, 2002.

'Roy of Siegfried and Roy Critical After Mauling.' CNN.com. 4 October
2003. <http://edition.cnn.com/2003/SHOWBIZ/10/04/roy.
attacked/>. Accessed 2 June 2012.

Shannon, Laurie. 'The Eight Animals in Shakespeare; or, Before the
Human.' *PMLA* 124.2 (2009): 472–79.

Singer, Peter. *Animal Liberation*. 1990. 2nd ed. London: Pimlico, 1995.

————, ed. *In Defence of Animals: The Second Wave*. Malden, MA:
Blackwell, 2006.

Stokes, John. '"Lion Griefs": The Wild Animal Act as Theatre.' *New
Theatre Quarterly* 20.2 (2004): 138–54.

Sukumar, Raman. *The Living Elephants: Evolutionary Ecology, Behavior, and
Conservation*. Oxford: Oxford UP, 2003.

Sunstein, Cass R., and Martha C. Nussbaum, eds. *Animal Rights: Current
Debates and New Directions*. Oxford: Oxford UP, 2004.

Tait, Peta. *Wild and Dangerous Performances: Animals, Emotions, Circus*.
Basingstoke, UK: Palgrave Macmillan, 2012.

Taylor, Paul. 'First Night: *The Wizard Of Oz*, London Palladium.'
Independent Online 2 March 2007. <www.independent.co.uk/arts-
entertainment/theatre-dance/reviews/first-night-the-wizard-of-oz-
london-palladium-2229689.html>. Accessed 14 May 2012.

Walker, Elaine. *Horse*. London: Reaktion, 2008.

Williams, David. 'Inappropriate/d Others: or, The Difficulty of Being a
Dog.' *The Drama Review* 51.1 (2007): 92–118.

Wolfe, Cary. *Animal Rites: American Culture, the Discourse of Species, and
Posthumanist Theory*. Chicago, IL: U of Chicago P, 2003.

————. *What Is Posthumanism?* Minneapolis: U of Minnesota P, 2010.

————, ed. *Zoontologies: The Question of the Animal*. Minneapolis: U of
Minnesota P, 2003.

Websites

Animal Asia. <www.animalsasia.org>. Accessed 3 June 2012.

High, Kathy. <www.embracinganimal.com>. Accessed 22 May 2012.

PAWS (Performing Animal Welfare Society). <www.pawsweb.org>. Accessed 3 June 2012.

UrbanPup. <www.urbanpup.com>. Accessed 14 May 2012.

index